WHEN THE LIGHT BREAKS THROUGH

Understanding Kundalini Experiences Through Psychology, Body, and Story

DANA SWAIN, PHD

ISBN: 978-1-950186-31-0

Cover and interior design by Jennifer Leigh Selig
Cover art by Jozef Klopacka

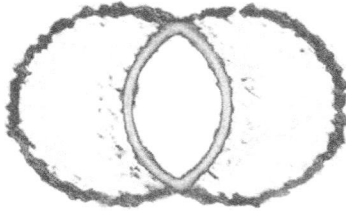

MANDORLA BOOKS
WWW.MANDORLABOOKS.COM

DEDICATION

In service and deep gratitude to the divine feminine in her form as Shakti-Kundalini, whose presence and grace has transformed my life.

TABLE OF CONTENTS

FOREWORD

The practice of kundalini is focused on understanding how the intrinsic power of consciousness expresses itself in manifestation. Kundalini is both the individuated expression of the Divine and the expression of that absolute power in all manifested form. Knowing this truth comes from the direct experience of that power as it flows through the veins of our awareness—psyche, mind, emotions, and body. In other words, it is the energy behind of all of those aspects of our being.

As this power is awakened, it is felt as energy pulsing throughout the channels and tributaries of our subtle body system. This movement of energy exposes the blocks and obstructions of our understanding and releases the dams of tension that prevent the free flowing vitality of the life force within us.

Kundalini meditation practice is the conscious directing of kundalini into the deeper dimensions of our being by directing kundalini into the internal subtle body and then expressing and engaging from that space in the world. This dynamic experience of interacting with our lives from an energetic rather than mental or emotional stance can transform our experience from one of "me and that" or "subject and object" to the deeper wisdom that everything is connected by its very existence. That is the revelation of the unity of life.

Practicing kundalini is the response to a deeper calling—the phone call from our deepest Self that says "I am here and I am you." This elicits a range of changes in our individual consciousness. In the infancy of our practice it allows us to process and transform the tensions and challenges and struggles of our life into the deeper understanding that our life happens on the field of our own awareness. All spiritual practice is meant to free us of misunderstanding. The maturation of the practice of kundalini is the freeing of God consciousness. It is the flood of insight that illuminates the highest truth. We can say that the true benefit of kundalini is the discovery of the profound joy and simplicity of life.

I recall the first time I met Dana (who I have named Samvitti, which translates to *she of infinite consciousness*). She came to my normal shakti transmission class, wherein the teacher transmits spiritual force through the eyes. When I looked at her it was like looking into a deep blue lagoon, full of depth and vibrancy. At the same time I sensed an asking for the fountainhead of that depth to be tapped so that it might perpetually fill her own awareness. When a teacher encounters that delicious hunger, all they can do is to prepare the banquet, to allow the "One Chef" to provide to ingredients to feed and nourish that person.

Although the awakening and liberation of kundalini has been an integral part of Indian/Asian culture for centuries, it is not relegated to any one culture or tradition. The authentic spiritual practices of these ancient civilizations have migrated to Western culture over the past 75 years, like flowing water that seeks new pathways on its way to the ocean. Because much of Western culture has enjoyed the freedom from the struggle to merely survive, it has become a ripe environment for the living spiritual energy of kundalini to establish itself and to blossom with earnest practitioners.

For almost 20 years Samvitti and I have shared that perpetually replenishing meal that is God's love. She has grown tremendously through her dedication, in-depth practice, willingness to be changed, and to serve the very energy that is giving her the capacity to do all those things. That compelled me to train and initiate her as an *acharya*—a teacher and lineage carrier of our wisdom tradition. She continues to serve with capacity, graciousness, and generosity.

Dana's truly insightful work is certainly part of that revelatory force of kundalini finding its own portal and expression. I applaud and bow to that.

Swami Khecaranatha
Spiritual Director, Heart of Consciousness

PREFACE

When I was twenty-three years old, I was going through a difficult time. I had ended a long-term relationship, moved to a new city, started graduate school, and had been physically assaulted by someone I thought I could trust. I felt alone, unsafe, and overwhelmed. I did my best to cope—I went to work every day, tried to stay emotionally engaged, and attempted to put the assault out of my mind.

It didn't work.

One day, alone in my apartment, I felt myself emotionally falling down a deep well. The picture of a well literally arose in my mind, and I tried in vain to grip onto the shallow, slippery shelves lodged intermittently on the walls. Somehow I knew these shelves were the rationales that I would have normally used as scaffolding to prop up my rational sense of self. But my rationalizing proved inadequate to the gravitational pull of the well, and down I fell until I hit the bottom, and everything—every thought, every feeling, and every sense of myself—went silent. The silence was so encompassing I thought I had literally died. But then I noticed I was still breathing.

In that moment of noticing my breath, an influx of what I can only describe as "presence" gently descended upon me in warm, calming waves. The presence had a distinctly feminine, profoundly loving quality to it, as if a mother was tucking a comforting blanket around me. With this presence as companion, I felt a deep peace. This was not the end of the experience, however, but only the beginning. For many months after, I experienced episodes of sweet bliss flowing through me, like nectar pouring into the open vessel of my body. By turns it was as viscous as honey or as hot as fire shooting through my veins, and always there was this sense of presence accompanying it.

Coincidentally, or perhaps it's more accurate to say synchronistically, during that time I met Olga Louchakova who was teaching a class on Christian Mysticism and Eastern Yoga at my graduate school, California Institute of Integral Studies. Intrigued, I signed up for the class. Olga was from Russia, with short blond hair and light green eyes. She talked of the experience of grace in the Eastern Orthodox religion and then spoke of the same energy in the Eastern philosophical traditions known as kundalini. My jaw dropped open—Olga was talking about the direct experience of grace or kundalini, and how it felt to a person experiencing it, in a manner that closely reflected my personal experience. Finally I had a name for what was happening to me! After class I related some of my experiences to her, and she extended an invitation to me to attend her private meditation classes, which I accepted. It was a relief to me that what I had experienced was well-known, documented, practiced, and systematized for thousands of years and by hundreds of thousands of people before me, most particularly within the wisdom lineage of Tantra. In this sense, I felt I had found my tribe.

I studied with Olga for seven years, practicing various forms of meditation. From the Eastern traditions I studied Vipassana and Dzogchen. I also practiced tuning into the subtle vibrations of my chakra system as well as the vibratory energy resonances within nature. These meditation practices helped me become aware of the subtle energy pulsations occurring in the body, and also had an impact on me psychologically: The more I worked with the energy within me, the more psychological work also surfaced, making it clear that what was happening on the spiritual level had an equally proportionate effect on the psychological level. This was the work of integrating spiritual insight with the shadow material of the unconscious, and living that dynamic interplay in everyday life. In a way, the work of the soul grounded the kundalini, and kundalini elevated and expanded my experience of living a soulful life.

The experiences of kundalini did not stay at a high level of intensity during these seven years. Kundalini would ebb and flow at varying levels of intensity over time, but I was always able to access the energy when I meditated. When I was twenty-nine, I ended another long-term relationship. After its termination, I was deeply drawn into a peaceful, nourishing solitude. My job as a trainer in high-tech had me traveling throughout the country alone for a month, and I spent my evenings in hotel rooms, reading Eastern philosophy and the Sufi poets Rumi and Hafiz. While I was evaluating another trainer on my last day of this month-long quiet introspection, I felt an electrical current run through my brain, from the left hemisphere to the right, and as it did so, my left eye seemed to see everything with only two dimensions, while my right eye observed the world in the normal three dimensions. I thought I might be having a stroke, but the sensation subsided within minutes. That evening, finally returning home and sleeping in my own bed, I woke up in the middle of the night with the sensation of the soles of my feet burning like they were on fire. They were so hot and prickly I got up to walk on the cool wooden floors. I wasn't clear at first that the heat running through my feet was kundalini. Wasn't kundalini supposed to just be in the chakras? The next night I woke up to a roaring sound like Niagara Falls running through me. Wherever I put my attention in my body, the roaring sound would come, and sometimes parts of my body—even an arm or a leg—would fill with light. I knew then that the kundalini energy was once again working to transform me in some unknown way. During the day, my words in conversation would often inexplicably become garbled midway through sentences like a momentary scrambling of a database. I found I could only eat a very simple, easily digestible diet.

At times I was emotionally and physically exhausted by what was occurring, but other times I was in a state of pure bliss. One Saturday while sitting in a café sipping a latte and reading poems by the Christian mystic Thomas Merton, my consciousness seemed to plunge into the poem, as if I had slipped through the cracks of the images and the words into timelessness, where I was no longer an individual, but part of the rhythmic rise and fall of cyclic epochs of time. The sense of beingness was not affected by time—it was beyond it. In an instant I was everything because I was nothing. It was a moment of realization: When we let go of our personal identity, we do not die, but rather, we become vast, we become all.

At some period during this kundalini process I began to experience the sensation of sweet droplets of nectar descending from the crown of my head into the center of my brain where the biological pineal gland is located. The sensation was of bliss so exquisite it was almost unbearable. After several weeks of going about my days with this phenomenon, there was an acceleration of experience. One evening during my meditation, the kundalini seemed to become tiny snakes racing through my nervous system, transforming it into light. Simultaneously, the kundalini ascended and descended my spine like a pump. As the energy ascended, it pounded the back of my head where the neck and skull meet like a fist, and with each strike my mind was engulfed in rapture. I was incapable of physical movement.

While the energy moved through me I had a vivid sense of 'knowing' that the body is worn like a coat for the soul. Upon death, it is simply taken off, but the soul consciousness of the person remains—not the personality, but something deeper and grander. I also had a clear image of the earth going through an evolution of consciousness via human consciousness, but this process was precarious, much like the dangers of giving birth, and it was necessary that people participate in this process of conscious evolution. After several months the energy quieted down again, and shortly after, I met my current teacher, Swami Khecaranatha (also referred to as Nathaji in this book), who teaches in the tradition of non-dual Tantric Shaivism.

So what do these transpersonal experiences have to do with regular life, with all its ecological, economic, and social crises? Why does it matter? Thomas Merton summed it up when he wrote:

> What can we gain by sailing to the moon if we are not able to cross the abyss that separates us from ourselves? This is the most important of all voyages of discovery, and without it, all the rest are not only useless, but disastrous.[1]

If we don't know ourselves at our very core, how can we act in the world without "disastrous" repercussions? In C. G. Jung's *Modern Man in Search of a Soul,* first published in 1933, Jung explored how the modern man, in losing his mythological and religious foundation, finds himself alienated from his own soul. James Hillman, Jungian analyst and the founder of archetypal psychology, took Jung's belief in the importance of connecting to one's deepest psychological and soulful roots a step further by suggesting we also need to connect to the soul of the world, the *anima mundi.* Both depth psychological and transpersonal approaches suggest that in order to successfully work to diminish the chasm of difficulties our global community currently faces, we must work with equal earnestness on our own psyches, the known parts and also the shadowy depths that lurk just underneath our awareness. And yet, it's not just our personal psyches that matter but also our collective psyche, with its cavernous archive of all human memory—the celebrated achievements and the repressed traumas. It may be that as we connect to that deep wellspring of vitality in ourselves and our collective humanity, we are then also able to better connect with the natural world we inhabit.

Kundalini is the light that explodes into insight beyond the threshold of limited self-identification, into the vast consciousness of everything, and I do mean everything. From that perspective the choices and actions we take may look very different from those we took when we saw ourselves, perhaps, as just a small, isolated person in a vast and indifferent world. Whenever and however we get a glimpse into an awareness of consciousness beyond our limited sense of ourselves, there is an organic shift which creates a space for spontaneous and joyful service to others. All of us have a genius that we can use and express as an offering of service and gratitude to that vital, creative Beingness that is expressed in every infinitesimal and immense aspect of our worldly experience.

If you are reading this you may have had an experience of, or are currently experiencing kundalini, and would like reassurance you are not losing your mind. You are not. Perhaps you wish to understand how to invite and then integrate this experience into your daily life, and you want to know more about how others have done so. Perhaps a friend or loved one is experiencing or has had experiences of kundalini, and has handed you this book or you sought it out, hoping to understand this phenomenon. You'll find that this book offers context to kundalini from a historical perspective, but equally as important, it shows how a few regular folks, myself included, have worked with kundalini while going about everyday life. I have found particularly helpful the depth psychological work of C. G. Jung and other Jungian and archetypal thinkers as a way to integrate my experience in a Western psychological framework. I offer it as a lens for viewing the experiences of kundalini and its integration when I share the in-depth stories of the four people I'm going to introduce you to.

Whether you are experiencing kundalini yourself or know someone who is, it's my hope this book can be of service to you, and to the rising light of your own divine Self.

PART ONE

KUNDALINI CONTEXT AND CONCEPTS

"Theologians may quarrel, but the mystics of the world speak the same language."
— *Meister Eckhart*

This book evolved out of my desire to integrate Eastern and Western perspectives to understand and work with kundalini. I wanted to express the internal landscape of these experiences, which can be so rich and beautiful and also unnerving when the experiences are unexpected and misunderstood. I wanted a variety of experiences of kundalini to be described in a grounded, easy-to-understand way, without losing touch with the beauty, bliss, and profound insight and awareness that accompanies kundalini.

I remember vividly how frightening and isolating it was to begin having experiences of kundalini when there was no framework in my North American culture for it. I didn't even have a name for it! While sharing my research for this book with others, I was surprised by the openness and curiosity people had for the subject, and even more surprised that after hearing some of the experiences shared in this book, many of those people suspected they might have had a glimmer of that same energy stirring in them at some period in their life. Often these experiences were not understood, or the fear of being crazy tamped down the energy. In fact, I regularly heard "I was afraid I was going crazy" from the people I spoke with. Our culture has pathologized not only kundalini but also many different types of mystical experiences, and so these experiences have gone underground; they have become almost unspeakable.

Recently, in a moment of unusual candor about kundalini in my own life, I found myself sharing some of my experiences with a group of women friends. They knew I practiced kundalini meditation, but I had never described any particular occurrence in detail. I took a deep breath, the same thought of "they're going to think I'm crazy" running through my head, and decided to be vulnerable and share a few deeply moving moments for me.

My friends listened with great respect and the room seemed pregnant with energy. Some of the women then shared their own spiritual experiences that they had never spoken of to anyone with the exception of perhaps one or two very close confidants. As each woman came forward with her own story, the space of storytelling became a sacred space, the words and experiences weaving an air of reverence around us. It created a deep connection and a sudden sense of intimacy between us, and even a kind of vital juiciness to the conversation.

I want more of those conversations to happen for people: to take our spirituality—not our religion or our beliefs—but our direct experience of the sacred, out of the closet. Sharing these experiences can feel more vulnerable, scary, and intimate than even talking about sexual or racial issues for some people. Yet that vulnerability is also an opening of the heart as well as of an expansion of knowledge and understanding of the wider possibilities available in our human life. It is my hope that such heart-opening spaces would elicit more compassion and understanding for all those going through spiritual processes both long and short term, so we are not alone and have support from friends, family, and community. I also hope that listening to or reading about such experiences sparks curiosity, and perhaps also elicits questions about our cultural perspectives that shun such a rich and essential aspect of being human.

For my research on this topic, which originated with my doctoral dissertation titled *Re-visioning Kundalini: Exploring Experiences of Kundalini from a Jungian and Archetypal Perspective*, I used the methodology of Organic Inquiry, which was developed in response to a need for a research approach that specifically addressed questions about spiritual dimensions of human experience, and also focused on the desire to attend to the research itself in a sacred way using a personal, accessible voice. In 1994, four researchers—Jennifer Clements, Dorothy Ettling, Dianne Jenett, and Lisa Shields—began to construct a methodology that met their desire to conduct research in a manner that engaged the whole person, using "feeling, intuitive, creative, and thinking modes" as equally fundamental tools not just for evaluating data, but also for expressing the results. Organic Inquiry's goal is for transformational learning and transformative changes of heart, for spiritual engagement and sacred embodiment.

Storytelling is part of our human DNA. Stories, both on a personal and collective level (which we sometimes call myth) connect us in profound ways. Each individual story with its particular details connects us to the universality of our human experience. Organic Inquiry's focus on storytelling was a good match with my degree program in depth psychology because both include mythology and spirituality as part of the psychology of the whole person. Depth psychology addresses transformational shifts in the psyche that are evidenced in dreams, synchronicities, and shadow material that must be integrated into individual consciousness for a truly lasting change and growth. Depth psychology also uses embodied and artistic methods when working with the psyche to access the imaginal and trans-rational realms of the unconscious that the rational, conscious mind often obscures.

In this book, five people, including myself, share their stories of kundalini, from their fear and their challenges to their awe and their gratitude. Together we inquired into our kundalini experience using dreams, embodied movement, journaling, and artistic methods, and I'll share those with you in these pages. Even though you haven't met any of us, I hope our stories strike a chord in you that resonates with your own experience, either as one who has experienced kundalini directly, or as someone curious about the experience. You'll notice our humanity, our emotions, our fears, and our awe as we attempt to understand and integrate our non-ordinary experiences into our ordinary, daily lives. None of us are saints—or even aspire to be. We are five people who found kundalini—or for some, kundalini found us—and we have chosen to work with the energy on a conscious, regular basis.

Kundalini is an experience that is available to everyone; it is extraordinary and also a part of our spiritual DNA. These stories are gifts offered from the heart, with the intention of promoting a deeper understanding of what kundalini experiences are like, how they are integrated, and the impact they can have on enriching our everyday lives. "Everyday lives" is just the tip of the iceberg of all that we can experience and know as human beings. Kundalini and the stories of the people experiencing it, points to the larger potential of consciousness that exists just beneath the surface of our conscious minds. This book and these stories are a deeper dive into that fascinating realm. I hope the stories serve you in your own psychological and spiritual growth.

CHAPTER ONE

What is Kundalini?

Kundalini is an innate, though often dormant, spiritual energy that resides in every human being. It is the power of consciousness, not just an individual rational consciousness, but cosmic and creative consciousness. When kundalini is firmly established, the experience is one of cosmic unity.

Kundalini has been known and experienced by people for thousands of years, and it is well-documented and accepted in Eastern cultures like India and the philosophies of Tantra and Tibetan Buddhism. It is described, though given different names, in other spiritual traditions throughout the world. The first written accounts of it are from Tantric texts dating back as early as the 4th century, and extensive documentation exists in the Shiva Sutras of the 9th century. Kundalini occurs in our modern, Western life as well. From my own observations, experiences of kundalini appear to be occurring with increasing frequency here in the West, a conclusion supported by scholars and kundalini practitioners such as Lawrence Edwards and Bonnie Greenwell.

As kundalini makes its ascension, the psyche—and by that I mean both the conscious and the unconscious mind—is transformed both psychologically and spiritually. Our behaviors, attitudes, and perspectives organically shift as unconscious material comes to light and hopefully becomes integrated. Our perspectives towards our relationship with others, with ourselves, and with the larger cultural community also naturally shifts into a resonance of loving kindness, compassion, and sense of being connected to a larger, more cosmic, universal sense of being.

People who experience kundalini activation in the West may not understand what is happening to them. Many Western psychological approaches have no framework to assist clients experiencing the effects of kundalini and may dismiss or misdiagnose an individual experiencing it as having a psychotic or schizophrenic episode. I believe these approaches don't always address the deeper dimensions of the psyche where transformations of the whole person can happen. When I refer to psychological transformation, I'll be coming from the perspective of Jungian depth psychology based on the foundational work of the Swiss psychologist C. G. Jung. I'll include insights from many depth psychologists who followed in Jung's footsteps and built on Jung's initial formulations.

Jung had a model of the psyche that expanded beyond the sense of the individual self, or ego consciousness. It included a sense of a "god-image" that the ego orbits. This "god-image" he named the Self with a capital S. In Indian philosophy, a similar distinction is made between the small self of the ego-mind and the Self that is one's true nature, and not separate from the divine. In his work, *Aion: Researches into the Phenomenology of the Self,* Jung wrote, "The spontaneous symbols of self, or of wholeness, cannot in practice be distinguished from a God-image . . . the 'renewal' of the mind is not meant as an actual alteration of consciousness, but rather as the restoration of an original condition."[2] The point that Jung is making here is that a renewal of mind, or psyche, when it is integrated with the Self, is not a totally new manifestation, but rather it is a restoration of wholeness. A Buddhist practitioner might say this is recognizing one's true nature. A Tantric practitioner might say it's recognizing the Self as oneself. I would say it is the experience of finally coming home to who we always knew we were, but have forgotten.

One additional term that I'll be using often throughout this book is "archetype." Jung took this word from the Greek word *arkhetupon* meaning an original pattern, and applied it to the psyche. Jung observed archetypal patterns occurring in the psyche of diverse groups of people, and he saw the same patterns in mythologies all over the world. Jung realized that the psyche was not just personal, but had a collective, transpersonal component as well, and this component went much deeper and farther than just the individual. The archetypes emerged as images in the psyche, and had a structuring effect on it. While there are many archetypes, the archetype of the Self is central, and is the unifying principle of wholeness.

So why is this important when we discuss kundalini? You might imagine kundalini as the archetypal energy of the Self. It's universal, it's transpersonal, it's collective, and it's also individualistic. We experience kundalini in our individual bodies as sensation, in our psyches as image/s, and on a transpersonal level, we experience it connecting us to others and to the transcendent.

When we talk about kundalini, we're talking about a subtle energy often called the subtle body, or the very refined and subtle energetic aspect of our biological system. When I refer specifically to the energy of kundalini, I will also often refer to its philosophical component of Tantra. I'll do this because Tantric texts are akin to reading technical how-to manuals of exceeding aesthetic beauty coupled with a profound worldview. The Tantric practitioners of ancient times didn't build a philosophical worldview based on mental conjecture. They wrote down their experiences working with the energy of kundalini, and the insights into consciousness that were revealed to them as they worked with the energy. Even though we might consider Tanta a religion, in actuality it's more like an investigative practice that reports back on the findings of the internal experience of consciousness and energy. So let's unpack the components of the energetic body according to the Eastern perspective.

Any discussion of kundalini necessitates a discussion of chakras, or wheels of subtle, vibratory energy that interpenetrate the physical body. As it rises, kundalini pierces and fully opens these vibratory centers during its ascent to ultimate unity with the macrocosmic force. In pictorial representation, these chakras appear as lotuses or mandalas, each with a corresponding image, animal, and letter denoting vibratory sound frequency, color, and element—all associated with a particular qualitative experience of consciousness associated with each chakra. I will go into a detailed description of these elements associated with each chakra, but it is important to note that the pictographic images you might see in books describing the chakras don't necessarily appear during the kundalini experience. That's because the images of chakras are symbolic of the vibration and energetic qualities of the chakra. Rather than thinking of chakras as one-dimensional wheels situated like pinpoints in the body, it may be more helpful to experience them directly and see what you notice. You might notice a spacious quality or a tight quality, and sense of openness or a sense of the chakra being dull or shut down. Some people see colors or feel the humming vibration of each chakra. Experiences will vary from person to person and from time to time. When working with kundalini regularly, the quality and sense of openness in the area of the chakra will shift as the chakra gradually opens. Jung felt that each chakra was like a mandala representing an entire archetypal world, and this is in accord with the Tantric view. What's interesting about the Tantric view is that by locating realms of consciousness within the body (and not just the brain), it acknowledges and assumes the importance of the role of the body—Tantra is a body-mind system as a whole, where the body has consciousness as well as the brain or the mind.

In fact, in the Tantric tradition, the body has far more than seven sites of consciousness. The entire corpus of the subtle body network includes the chakras, the three main channels of *ida, pingala,* and *sushumna,* and 72,000 other *nadis,* or energy conduits existing throughout the body. The ida channel resides in the left side of the body. It's considered to be feminine energy, and begins in the first chakra at the base of the spine, terminating in the left nostril. The pingala channel resides in the right side of the body. It's considered masculine energy, and begins in the first chakra at the base of the spine, and terminating in the right nostril. The ida and pingala channels cross at the sushumna, the central energy channel of the body, at each chakra location. This subtle body network is thought to be the driving force that informs the mental and emotional body, and is the point of emergence of the physical body.

You may be familiar with the seven chakra centers co-existing with the physical body, but allow me a quick review. Beginning at the base of the spine, the first chakra, called the *Muladhara* or root chakra, is imaged as a lotus with four red petals, and corresponds to the element of earth, and the mantra—or sound frequency—*Lam.* It is here that kundalini lies in its dormant state. The second chakra is called *Svadishtana* and is associated with the genital and pelvic region. Its image is of a lotus flower with six petals, and corresponds with the element of water and the mantra *Vam.* The third chakra is called *Manipura* and is situated in the navel area. It is pictured as a blue lotus of ten petals and is related to the element of fire and the mantra *Ram. Anahata* is the fourth chakra, associated with the region of the heart, the element of air, and the mantra *Yam.* The fifth chakra is called *Visuddha* and is located in the throat region. Its lotus has sixteen petals of dark purple and its mantra is *Ham.* The *Ajna* is the sixth chakra, commonly referred to as the "third eye," and is located between the eyebrows, though this also signifies that it is within the skull region as well. Its corresponding lotus is white with two petals and its mantra is *Om.* It is associated with cognitive mental powers. The seventh chakra, *Sahasrara,* is the ultimate culmination of all the integrated chakras beneath it. It is represented as a lotus of one thousand petals and is located a few inches above the crown of the head—some say it interpenetrates the crown of the skull. This is where the full integration of kundalini is experienced. Each chakra also has corresponding letters and deities associated with it. Further details of the chakra images can be found in many original and modern Tantric sources and commentary, including *The Tantric Way,* by Ajit Mookerjee and Madhu Khanna.

In another book by Ajit Mookerjee, titled *Kundalini: The Arousal of Inner Energy,* the author compares the activation of the chakras and the rise of kundalini to Jung's individuation process, the process of coming to wholeness, to the Self. Mookerjee noted that while for Jung the process of individuation is complete when the thinking, feeling, sensing, and intuiting functions are balanced, so it is that each chakra and corresponding element is a new quality of consciousness that is first achieved, then integrated, and finally enfolded into the next, increasingly refined chakra. But this process is not necessarily linear, like climbing a ladder from one chakra rung to the next. Kundalini moves with its own kind of intelligence, nibbling away at physical, emotional, and mental tensions. With each new release of tension comes new insight, new understanding, and an expanded sense of consciousness. Thinking of kundalini as dialectical in nature—working in energetic conversation with the psyche and body—is akin to Jung's concept of the conscious aspects of the psyche being in a dialectical conversation with the emerging aspects of the unconscious as they appear in dreams and complexes, in order to resolve and integrate oppositional psychic forces.

Western science and culture have historically had a tendency to ignore or disregard as invalid the experiences of the subtle body and realms of more subtle consciousness. There have been exceptions, which I'll point out later in this book, but for now I hope you have an image of the structure of the subtle body and kundalini, and how it interpenetrates all aspects of our being from the physical, emotional, and mental, to touch on realms of knowing that are not often addressed in Western culture. In the next chapters I'll focus on how kundalini impacts those different realms of the psyche as it progresses through us.

In Chapter Two, we'll look at the historical and cultural underpinnings of kundalini. I'll offer a sampling of where kundalini is known in other cultures, albeit under different names. We'll take a look at Eastern and Western approaches to the concept of alchemy—the transformation of material matter and the internal matters of the spirit— and I'll discuss its psychological importance for Jung, and for the process of kundalini awakening.

Chapter Three will explore how kundalini impacts the body, both the physical body as well at the subtle body, and look at some of the recent studies in science on the physiological changes that occur in the physical body when kundalini is active. We'll dip into the wider view on how kundalini might be a fractal, an individual component that mirrors a larger systemic change in the natural systems of nature and the cosmos.

Chapter Four focuses on the psychological impact of kundalini from both the Western psychological perspective, particularly Jung's, and from the perspective of Eastern philosophy, most particularly Tantra. We'll explore the analogues of similarity between the two perspectives and also where they diverge. I'll suggest that kundalini engenders a quality of conscious that is more Eros in quality, rather than a more Logos consciousness, and I'll offer the Greek god Dionysus as a metaphor to explain the often unusual and uncontrollable onset of kundalini for the individual.

If you prefer to dive right into the stories of kundalini, then feel free to skip the rest of Part One, which is more academic in nature, and go directly to Part Two. In Part Two you'll find five stories from my research on kundalini, including how each person embraced and integrated their experience into everyday life. You can return to Part One any time if you want contextual information. I encourage you to read in a manner that suits your needs and satiates your curiosity most deeply.

CHAPTER TWO

Historical and Cross-Cultural Perspectives on Kundalini

The kundalini experience, as I mentioned in our last chapter, is an ancient phenomenon. The scholar and Indologist Georg Feuerstein wrote that kundalini experiences are probably as old as humanity's engagement with spiritual dimensions of our being, though it was first in Tantra that experiences were written down and codified. In this chapter, I've selected examples of how kundalini has been described or encountered in other cultures and times. It's not meant to be exhaustive in scope, but I hope it gives you a sampling of the depth and breadth of the phenomenon of kundalini throughout human history. When I first experienced kundalini, it was immensely helpful to know that I was not alone and not losing my mind. The framework of a tradition that was thousands of years old, with its practices and the documentation of others' experiences, relieved my anxiety and transformed it into curiosity. What could the people who came before me, some thousands of years before me, teach me about what was happening to me and what it meant for my life? My curiosity has lasted more than 25 years.

The historian of religion Mircea Eliade noted that in geographically and culturally diverse religions, the image of the central pole, or *axis mundi*, which delineated sacred space from mundane space, was common. The axis mundi represented the sacred center of the world, allowing access to transcendent realms while also allowing the sacred transcendent space to penetrate the mundane realms. Through this pole the three cosmic levels of earth, heaven, and underworld were all connected. The axis mundi as the sacred center of the world was symbolized in nature in forms such as a tree or a sacred mountain, in cities as the central circle or pole at the center of the city, and in the home as the central pole that was part of many architectural constructs. Eliade pointed out that for our ancestors, it was crucial to live as close to the center of the sacred world as possible. This center was not only an external reality but also an interiorly known experience, because the axis mundi also existed within the body as the spinal column. The sacred cosmos dwelled within through the central axis of the spinal column, and therefore, the body also reflected the cosmos. The body was an individualized mirror or the macrocosmic universe and as such shared a sense of sanctity with the transcendent realms. Eliade referred to this cosmological system as the "Body-House-Cosmos."

Eliade also noted that images of the axis mundi in varying cultures always had, or were capable of having an opening in the body—usually through the top of the head—that allowed for passage to other worlds, including the passage of the soul in death by way of the crown of the head. Eliade used Tantra and the Indian Vedic tradition as the most demonstrative examples of this symbolic representation, which described the *brahmarandhra*, or the top of the head and crown chakra, where the soul leaves the body at the time of the body's death.

Traditionally, kundalini has been depicted as the sacred microcosmic energy lying dormant at the base of the spine (which one might consider the underworld of the body) that rises up through the spine to not only reach, but transcend the crown chakra and thereby come into union with the macrocosmic divine, cosmic energy. While Tantra called this axis mundi the *sushumna*, the symbolic representation and significance is the same. The body was included in the continuum of the sacred realms of the cosmos.

Besides the axis mundi, another key image in kundalini iconography is the caduceus, which is an image of a central pole or channel with two snakes intertwining at specific points on the central channel from the bottom to the top. The caduceus in the West is also a symbol associated with the Greek god Hermes, and is still commonly used as a symbol for Western medicine. But the symbol of the caduceus has been found as far back as the Sumerian culture. The scholar Thomas McEvilley, in his book *The Shape of Ancient Thought: Comparative Studies in Greek and Indian Philosophy,* wrote that the caduceus as a motif was first discovered in Sumerian iconography, in such artwork as the Gudea Vase, dated to 2150 BCE. He noted that the caduceus image did not appear again in the Indus Valley until over a millennium later. He made the important additional observation that whether this image from Sumerian times has similar philosophical or religious connotation as that of Tantric texts describing kundalini is not known, but regardless, he believed it worthy of note that even in this ancient Sumerian image, the serpents intertwine at seven points along the pole—points that coincide with the seven chakras in the kundalini Tantric system.

Other ancient cultures have writings on the phenomena of kundalini, but named and described it within their particular cultural context. According to scholar Edward Bynum, in his book *Dark Light of Consciousness*, in pre-Islamic Egypt, called Kemet, there was a similar energy and spiritual practice to India's yoga. In Kemet, this energy was known as the *arat sekhem*. Practices of working with arat sekhem included specific breathing techniques, working with body positions and sound, and meditating. The purpose of these practices was to bring together the world of the spirit and the world of the body, which were symbolized as the Upper and Lower Kingdoms of Egypt. Similarly, the Tantric tradition also included the physical practices of yoga, its various forms including practices of body postures, sound work called *mantra*, and breath work called *pranayama*, by which this union between microcosm and macrocosm might be attained.

At least part of Tantra's lineage derived from early Eastern indigenous and shamanistic practices, and slowly evolved over time into a sophisticated religion. Other shamanistic and indigenous cultures report similar experiences to those described in Tantra about kundalini. For example, ethnologist Lorna Marshall worked with the !Kung bushmen in Africa. Marshall noted that the !Kung described an experience called *ntum* that materialized in ritualized trance-inducing dance. The dancers reported that the ntum moved up their spines and they lost their normal senses, often going into a deep trance and becoming semi or fully unconscious.

In another example of this perspective, transpersonal psychologist Bonnie Greenwell thoroughly elucidated cross-cultural examples of the kundalini experience in her book *Energies of Transformation: A Guide to the Kundalini Process*. Greenwell referenced the work of Frank Waters who argued that the Hopi Native Americans knew of kundalini in their own cultural setting. According to Waters, the Hopi believed that the human body and the body of the earth were created in a similar manner. Each had an axis running through it. Humanity's axis was the backbone while the earth had a rotational axis. According to Greenwell, the Hopis also believed that at the top of the head there was a portal through which one could connect with the Creator. This was also the doorway through which the soul passed upon death of the body.

Another common symbol and experience of kundalini is that of light. Physiologically one may experience the energy of kundalini throughout the body and particularly through the spinal column that often coalesces with internal visionary experiences of light. Similarly, the philosophy of Taoism focuses its practices on the circulation of this light as a way to transform the entire body and mind of the practitioner.

The well-known Taoist work *The Secret of the Golden Flower* has many translations from Chinese into other languages. It was originally translated from Chinese into German, and introduced to Western readers by the sinologist Richard Wilhelm in the 1920s. In an online version entitled *The Secret of the Golden Flower: A Chinese Book of Life,* attributed originally to Wang Chongyang, this English translation describes methodologies of cultivating the energy and light to balance the dark and light poles within the body. These energies were also called *yin* and *yang,* and correlate to the ida and pingala channels in Tantric practices. Through earnest and prolonged focus on energetic exercises in the correct manner, the practitioner can gain the Elixir of Life, the liquid of immortality. The idea of an Elixir of Life or attainment of an immortal, incorruptible body, known in Western alchemy as the philosopher's stone, is an idea commonly shared by many cultures in the Middle Ages, and also pertains to practices surrounding kundalini. In fact, Tantra reached its height of popularity during the same time period as other esoteric alchemical traditions, and it's worth taking a closer look at this historical period to highlight the close connections between Eastern and Western alchemical traditions.

Multicultural Alchemy

It was through Jung's exposure to Wilhelm's translation of *The Secret of the Golden Flower* that his interest in alchemy was ignited. In medieval times, alchemy was thought to be a way to turn base metals into gold. On a metaphysical level, the alchemist would also transform via the wisdom he gained. The wisdom was often called "the philosopher's stone." For Jung, Western alchemy held potential correlates within its symbolic framework to his formulation of psychic development in analytical psychology. It seemed to Jung that though the alchemists were working with metals, on another level they were projecting their psychology unto those metals, thus refining their psyche as they worked to refine the metal. Though Jung chose to steep himself in the lineage of Western alchemy, he acknowledged similar alchemical traditions in Eastern cultures in several of his writings. It is a worthwhile endeavor to develop a picture of the geographical locations and ambiance of the medieval time period—which was the heyday of alchemical thought and practice—in order to see how closely these purportedly separate schools of alchemical thought were actually linked.

In the early centuries of the medieval period, there was a significant amount of cultural engagement between India and Greece, often through the cosmopolitan and culturally diverse country of Persia and the Persian Empire. According to scholar Thomas McEvilley in his book *The Shape of Ancient Thought*, the Persian Empire employed Greek mercenary soldiers into the fourth century, and trade routes remained open via waterways. It may have been through this route that Indian yogis came to Greece to talk with the prominent philosophers of the time. Persian courts often hosted both Greek and Indian people of importance, and an atmosphere of intellectual inquiry and exchange would have been present. A transfusion of cultural philosophies, religions, and science most likely transpired between the Indian and Greek cultures through the geographical channel of the Persian Empire.

McEvilley referred specifically to fragments of various works written by the ancient Greek philosopher Heraclitus that might demonstrate the infusion of Indian thought with Greek thought. Heraclitus wrote on the nature of change using imagery of the elements from fire, water, and earth as metaphors for the process of the soul entering and leaving human form. Heraclitus' exposition is significantly similar to the writing in the Indian Upanishads, particularly to *the Cha' ndogya*, also called the *Doctrine of the Five Fires*. Although the Upanishads predate written texts of Tantra, it is apparent in Heraclitus' work and the Upanishads' use of elemental imagery and it correlates to the soul's passage through time: earth, water, fire. These are also common metaphorical and actual elements descriptively used in Western alchemy.

One particular text, the *Timaeus*, attributed to Plato, acts as a kind of Rosetta Stone connecting Indian thought with Greek thought and demonstrating how alchemical concepts actually were blended. The *Timeaus* is a creation story that depicts an origin of chaos that comes into order over time through the will of a kind of cosmic architect who not only creates the entire cosmos, but also creates each specific element, including humans, as a reflection that mirrors the cosmos. The soul of the human being desires to be reconnected and reunited with the soul of the world, and one of the ways to execute this experience of reunification, at least for men, is through the sublimation of sexual desire or power and the cultivation of semen in order to direct its symbolic power (which is the power of the soul) upwards through the spinal column and into the brain, which was considered the location of the higher soul. The brain and the penis were connected via the circuit, or route, of the spinal column, which is a similar notion and practice described in Chinese alchemy, or Taoism, and in Western and Eastern Indian alchemy. The similarities between the *Timaeus* and the written work on kundalini in the Hindu system are striking. The *Timaeus* describes in detail how the body was created and a more subtle body, including two channels on the left and right side of the body on either side of the spine, which weave through each other and cross at specific points in the body—these seem to correspond to the ida and pingala in Tantric texts. Although Plato's description of the body and internal organs is very specific and accurate throughout the text, these two channels cannot be accounted for as part of the physiology of the physical body. It can be suggested then that the notion of these subtle body channels may have as their source—or at least have been influenced by—the Indian traditions and texts that include descriptions of the subtle body channels, which predate Greek writings with similar elements.

The Inner and Outer Aims of Alchemy

Jung's extensive studies of ancient alchemical texts and images convinced him that the alchemists were not just working with matter to turn it into gold, but were simultaneously projecting their psychology onto matter, working as much with the contents of their psyches as they were with earth-based material. On a psychological level, the objective—or the *opus magnum* as it was called—was not simply to turn matter into gold, but to foster and create the gold of an illuminated mind, the distillation of baser instincts into a refined substance that freed one from lower instincts, desires, and cravings, while simultaneously redeeming nature from its imperfect, unconscious state. For Jung, as alchemists explored nature, they were simultaneously projecting unconscious material of the psyche onto matter so that the contents of the unconscious might also be revealed and understood. Jung noted that these projections were entirely unconscious to the alchemists, as are the nature of all psychological projections.

After prolonged immersion into many alchemical works, Jung concluded that alchemy was a predecessor and lineage link to his own psychology and his understanding of the unconscious, both collective and personal. He saw the processes of alchemy as akin to the processes of individuation. Alchemy's images and affect-laden stages and its attempt to reconcile opposites, worked to bring all disparate and unacknowledged aspects of the psyche into union, and resonated with what Jung experienced for himself and observed in his clients as they struggled with bringing their psychological complexes into accord.

For the Indian alchemist, the terrain of transmutation from baser to finer substances happened within the landscape of the body. Both aimed at purifying impure elements and transforming them into the gold of immortality, but the Indian alchemist used the psychophysical body, and the Western alchemist attempted to achieve the same results using projection of psychic contents onto matter.

Just as Jung observed and worked with alchemical imagery presented to him by client dreams, Indian alchemy in the form of Tantric practices has its very practical applications. The entire Indian alchemical opus consisted of a medicinal aspect called *Ayurveda*, a physical regime of strength and purification called *Hatha-yoga*, and a meditative aspect that worked with the subtle body and the kundalini energy.

The scholar David Gordon White described the correlation between the yogic medicine tradition and the mineral elements and symbolism expressed in most alchemical systems. According to White:

> Gold is identified with earth, lead with water, copper with fire, iron with air, and zinc with ether. In hatha yoga, the raising of the yogins' energy, figured as the female kundalini serpent, through the system of the cakras [sic], also effects a reabsorption of gross into subtler elements . . . As in Samkhya, hatha yoga, and the other hierarchical systems, so too in alchemy: that which is higher encompasses, absorbs, that which is lower.[3]

The chakras themselves are identified with mineral elements, and as the chakras are purified and refined, so are the elements within the structure of the psycho-spiritual system. While in some Indian doctrines there is an emphasis away from the worldly, embodied life in favor of asceticism and transcendence, in the Tantric tradition, which is essentially synonymous with Indian alchemy, there is the pursuit of higher states through ascension of kundalini through the chakras. The whole Tantric system is one that sees life as a continuum of energy from grosser forms and resonances to higher, more subtle vibratory resonance. The lower reality is not separate from the higher reality. At its core is the same subtle vibration that could be discovered through the purification of the denser, lower frequencies. Thus, the main thrust and theme of Tantra is integration—the individual self with the sense of a cosmic self, and the physical body embedded within a spiritual existence.

Whether externally or internally oriented, similar themes seem to be present in both Eastern and Western alchemy: elements of the earth are correlated with color and mineral substances, such as red to the mineral substance mercury. There is a movement towards integration of male and female principles (such as yin and yang, Shakti and Shiva), and a death and resurrection of a mortal body for an immortal one, which can be understood to be both literal and metaphorical in meaning. These similarities seem to suggest that the alchemical images and processes are cross-cultural and archetypal, and may therefore manifest in any individual through dream images and themes, psychological processes, and physical affects. I suggest that the archetypal process of kundalini continues to occur in individuals, regardless of their cultural background, precisely because it is an archetypal experience of psychological and spiritual growth. In other words, kundalini experiences manifest for Westerners in our times, even without studying or knowing anything about either Eastern or Western traditions of alchemy and Tantra, so understanding these experiences better and integrating them into the personality as part of the individuation process becomes a powerful way to affect healing and transformation.

If these meanderings through the thicket of time, philosophical thought, and varying cultural perspectives has left you feeling a bit lost, here's a summary of what is most significant in these last two chapters:

1. Kundalini has been known and experienced in many different

cultures. Though it is best known and documented in Eastern philosophical traditions, most specifically that of Tantra, the essence of it is a human experience regardless of culture or historical time period.

2. There is significant evidence to suggest the concept of kundalini came from the East, particularly India, but was shared with the West. This occurred most significantly in Persia, which was a geographic area of great cultural diversity, particularly in the 11th and 12th century. Therefore, one can see evidence of kundalini in Greek written work such as the *Timeaus*.

3. Both Eastern and Western cultures practiced alchemy. In the West, alchemy was about changing base metals into gold, but also held the esoteric significance of spiritual transformation. In the East, the alchemical transformation occurred in the body. A purified body reflected pure divinity (as in the adage, *as above so below*), and igniting kundalini was one way to purify the fleshly body into a divine body.

4. Jung saw similarities between Western alchemy and his own analytical psychology, with the shared goal of the transformation of the whole psyche over time.

5. One can see both in Eastern and Western alchemy some overlapping notions of alchemical and spiritual transformation. There is an archetypal dimension to both alchemy and to psycho-spiritual transformation, but one doesn't need to know about alchemy or history to experience this transformation, or to experience kundalini. Many people in the West do experience kundalini, even if they don't know what it is. But knowing that kundalini is a universal, archetypal experience can help a person to integrate the experience in a way that is healing and trans-formative.

CHAPTER THREE

Psyche and Matter:
Kundalini in the Physical and Subtle Body

Experiencing the physical symptoms of kundalini can be the most disconcerting aspect of the process, particularly in the West where historically there has been little or no cultural context for such experiences. Often what immediately follows a physical experience of kundalini activation is a feeling of concern for our sanity or worry that something has gone awry with an aspect of our health. As an example, I once lead a meditation class consisting of a guided meditation through the chakras. At the end of the class, I reminded the participants to be mindful of their emotional states, to be gentle with themselves the rest of the day, and to pay attention to their dreams. One woman, Colleen, whom I had not previously met (but who you will meet in more detail in the stories of Part Two), came to her first class and afterwards had the following experience which she described to me in an email and is shared here with her permission:

> Yesterday afternoon I had a major, joyful breakthrough around fear and letting go. Then I moved on with my day and all felt normal. Last night though, I was revved up, like a caffeine high without the jitters. I normally go to sleep at nine; it was well after one a.m. when I tried to force myself to sleep. This is most unusual. Lying in bed, I felt completely awake. I was irritated because I knew I had to get some rest but I wasn't tired. I became aware of a large pillar/tube of incredibly powerful pulsating energy in my "space," perpendicular to me running from up high down

into the ground. Mind blowing. Eventually, about 20% of me felt really tired yet another part was saying, "Whoa! What is this? Watch this. 'Pay attention!" I thought I might be having some kind of reaction to the new antibiotic that I started at ten p.m., frankly. I wouldn't call it hallucinating but it is definitely something I have never experienced before. Eventually I shut my left eye and part of me was sleeping. My right eye and a greater part of "me" was awake watching this energy move. It was wild. Scary. Fascinating. What the heck!?! One eye closed and one open? Part sleeping, part awake?? Then I remembered you said we might have some interesting experiences and I felt reassured.

In this situation, I offered her the simple reassurance after the experience that she was not losing her mind, and I normalized the experience by naming the physical effects as common kundalini manifestations. This put Colleen at ease and she felt more comfortable just going along with the process.

Why is the body—subtle and gross—so important to any thorough examination of the individuation or enlightenment process? The Buddhist scholar and teacher Reginald Ray, in his book *Touching Enlightenment,* made an interesting observation. "To approach the world by objectifying it, to reside mainly in the head, is to put ourselves in a position of domination, mastery and control. We domesticate the world by filtering it through our concepts, and this enables us to own and possess it, to make it subservient to our agendas and wants."[4]

I agree with Ray. If we remain in a conceptual, analytical framework when studying differing levels of consciousness and psycho-spiritual growth, we limit what may actually be present or organically occurring by cordoning off phenomenological reality to pre-constructed conceptual frameworks. In doing so, we risk sequestering and subtly manipulating reality into what is palatable or acceptable to our conscious opinions and desires.

Ray eloquently noted that "to be in the body is to know our sense perceptions as opening out into a sacred world . . . Somehow the body's knowledge is so much more subtle, but also so much more convincing and satisfying than knowledge that is purely conceptual."[5] According to Ray, the body does not—even cannot—tell a lie. It responds truthfully and elegantly to what it encounters or experiences and it cannot create artificial boundaries—that happens in the mental sphere. The body is an open system, interacting and reacting to its environment, and it functions outside of the range of our rational consciousness, with the latter's tendency towards control and a bounded sense of reality. When addressing experiences of kundalini, it is clear that the body plays a major role in expressing and responding to the subtle and yet often overwhelmingly dominant energy coursing through it. The sensing body makes the experience present, real, immediate, and immanent. Mental conceptions and expectations often crumble in the face of such clear physical feedback even though we may not understand what our experience means, or what to expect from our bodies next. Therefore, it is important to attempt to address the body and the subtle body on its own terms, without jumping to conceptual, philosophical, or psychological conclusions prior to first noting what is actually happening within the subtle and physical body, and to stay open to treasures that may surface through a grounded exploration.

Jung had a fascination with Eastern practices and psychology, but also held trepidation for Westerners practicing them, suggesting that no Westerner had the patience for it, and these experiences might actually lead to madness. From our view in the 21st century with yoga studios and meditation practices abounding, Jung's concern seems dated and rather inconsequential. Regardless of whether practices that might induce kundalini awakening are "good" or not, experiences of kundalini occur even without the study or practice of Eastern techniques. Kundalini experiences seem to have correlations with near-death experiences, they sometimes occur as a result of using hallucinogenic drugs, they can arise from physical or emotional stress or trauma, and occasionally seem to appear without any external causal factor. This would imply that the phenomenon of kundalini is not an experience happening only in particular cultural contexts, but it is a potential phenomenon for all human beings, and having a kundalini experience may be grounded and integrated better by understanding that it is a universal human experience, and Westerners too can find ways to work with the energy that are useful in our own cultural context.

Modern Scientific Approaches to Kundalini

Since the latter half of the 20th century and continuing into the present day, the physiological aspects of kundalini have been studied by a small group of medical doctors and scientists. Lee Sannella was one of the first medical doctors to study kundalini phenomenon from a phenomenological and physiological perspective. Sannella's accounting of his findings is documented in his book *The Kundalini Experience: Psychosis or Transcendence?*, and has gained wide readership for those interested in the subject of kundalini. Sannella's research was based solely on the physical phenomenon, rather than emotional or thought processes, or experiences of energy that seemed vague to him. He pointed out that though Jung defined himself as an empirical scientist, Jung still approached religious experience "principally through comparative analysis rather than rigorous personal experimentation or laboratory testing of suitable volunteers." Sannella additionally contended that there was room for both approaches, but focused on the body as equally important to the mind, as both body and mind "form a dynamic unity or are polar aspects of a larger reality."[6]

Sannella categorized the physical affects of kundalini to include experiences that involved a sense of heat and/or cold, experiencing internal light or sounds, varying amounts of pain throughout the body, emotional and mental or thought disruptions, indications of detachments and disassociated cognitive states, "single seeing and the great body,"[7] where one may see out of a single eye (rather than both) or experience the body to feel gigantic, and out of body or psychic experiences. These physiological aspects are also supported by the findings of Yvonne Kason, Bonnie Greenwell, Stanislav Grof, and well documented by the personal experiences of Gopi Krishna.

While both Sannella and Grof pointed out that Taoist or Chinese yoga referred to an energy current running throughout the body in a circulatory motion, and even initiating in the left big toe, this is not in conflict with the Tantric description, where the 72,000 nadis circulate throughout the body. One of my own experiences that heralded an extended and dramatic kundalini arousal originated with heat at the bottom of my feet; however, it was not until the kundalini reached the chakras that psychological patterns erupted to the surface of my consciousness. The Tantric perspective focuses on the chakra centers because these centers, in addition to being loci of vibrational energy, are also archetypal levels of personal and collective unconscious material that must be acknowledged and integrated in order to experience the totality of consciousness. According to Indologist Lilian Silburn, the chakra centers hold knots, called *granthis*, of condensed energy that bind an individual to a narrow sense of ego consciousness. Silburn described these knots as

> unconscious complexes (*samskara*) . . . Each knot, being an obstruction, must be loosened so that the energy released by the centers can be absorbed by kundalini and thus regain its universality. These wheels are by no means physiological and static centers of the gross body, but centers of power belonging to the subtle body, centers that the yogin alone, during the unfolding of kundalini, can locate with as much accuracy as if they belonged to the body.[8]

Similar to Jung's conception of archetypal forces within the psyche, kundalini is one of the energetic instigators in the revelation of the totality of human potential, or recognition of the indwelling divine within. But this revelation includes the polarity of psychic density and shadow material that must be recognized and resolved. Scholar and medical doctor Olga Louchakova, a contributor to the book *Kundalini Rising*, described the path of kundalini as a movement of returning to the self and as such the process of the return contains the contrasting tensions in the psyche between the spirit attempting to unveil the truth of itself within the limited, mortal material of the body. The body also participates in the process of spiritual maturation, acting as an instrument and expression of the challenges and triumphs of the process itself. Louchakova also observed that "what kundalini can unearth in the body/subtle body system are very deep patterns in the structure of the psyche that go beyond personal narrative but penetrate into culturally held values and even collective patterns and trauma."[9] Although kundalini is considered a subtle body phenomenon that often affects the physical body, it also may affect and unearth deep psychological complexes, which suggest the link between the body and the psyche.

Jungian scholar Veronica Goodchild, in her essay, "Psychoid, Psychophysical, P-Subtle! Alchemy and a New Worldview," wove together concepts of the subtle body with Jung's understanding of Western alchemy and its relevance to psychological stages in the individuation process. For Goodchild, the stages in Western alchemy are processes of "making spirit matter and matter psyche" and while the psyche undergoes this conversion, it creates the subtle body and strengthens the subtle body, which she called the third body, which is both matter and spirit. This third body is "symbolized by various images such as the *filius*, the divine or gold child, the philosopher's stone, the elixir, the golden germ."[10] I would suggest that the alchemical filius, the elixir, "*aqua vitae*," and the philosopher's stone are all names that can be considered not only metaphorical images of psychological transmutation, but that the phenomenological reality of these named substances is in fact kundalini. Kundalini, I would argue, is the third thing, the "stuff" of the subtle body, which is the driving impetus that propels the psyche to its telos of wholeness. Goodchild noted that Jung, in his *Nietzsche Seminars*, wrote on the subtle body as "a body formed out of suffering intense affect and emotions that burn up superfluities, according to the alchemists—as a kind of invisible somatic unconscious."[11] In other words, for Jung, the subtle body was created by the work of coming to terms with our tensions and misunderstandings, of resolving our complexes, which in turn help us to integrate the archetypal energies latent in the unconscious.

Marie-Louise von Franz addressed alchemy and the connection between psyche and matter in her book *Psyche and Matter*. She noted that the human body "is composed of the same elements as the macro-cosmos," and it is through working with the body that one can come to understand the greater mystery of the extension of a living presence within matter. For von Franz, this discovery did not come by projecting consciousness onto matter, as Jung suggested the early alchemists did, "but through meditative introspection, through sinking down into the endosomatic psychic feelings and sensations."[12]

Such processes of emotional and physical affect certainly resonate with the reported experiences of those going through a kundalini process. Kundalini may be considered the elixir that spiritualizes matter and the body, infusing the mundane with the sense of numinosity. External to the body, kundalini is also referred to as *Shakti* or the divine feminine and dynamic principle that is the diverse manifestation of material reality. Shakti is not considered separate from kundalini, and this points to Jung's own conception of the spectrum of the archetypal forces from the unknowable level of basic biological instinct, through nature and the collective and personal unconscious, and into the imaginal, mythical realms.

To experience kundalini through the body and the personal to the impersonal and imaginal realms is to experience what Jung referred to as the *third coniunctio*, which is the experience of an individual psyche coming into union with the *unus mundus*, or the underlying ontological totality of being. In working with images and texts of alchemy, Jung noted that the psychological and alchemical processes are not immaterial, but make up the subtle body, which he called "semi-spiritual in nature." Indian Tantra might use the images of chakras to denote this subtle realm, while alchemy had a gestalt of other images, yet both types of images cannot be seen as merely metaphorical, but as archetypally symbolic images pointing to something perhaps perceptually immaterial but suffused with an entirely experiential sense of a "real" realm and sense of being. According to Jung in his work *Psychology and Alchemy*:

> When physics touches on the "untrodden, untreadable regions," and when psychology has at the same time to admit that there are other forms of psychic life besides the acquisitions of personal conscious—in other words, when psychology too touches on an impenetrable darkness—then the intermediate realm of subtle bodies comes to life again, and the physical and the psychic are once more blended in an indissoluble unity.[13]

One might conjecture that Jung knew of this realm through direct experience throughout his life, but the apex may have been the time of his confrontation with the unconscious after his break with Freud, which is documented in Jung's *The Red Book*. These experiences of the intermediate realm of subtle bodies also occur for people experiencing kundalini awakenings, and can be deeply disconcerting as well as profoundly compelling. One experience I had which seems to typify the "realness" of this other realm of the subtle body occurred several years ago during a meditation retreat. As I was meditating, I experienced the energy that normally flows upwards turn into what can only be described as a metal rod running vertically through the center of my torso. My sense of self became situated inside the rod, where I experienced myself as pure consciousness, and yet I was aware that my "little self," or the self that I was in the habit of identifying with, was floating a little away from my body, connected to this larger "Self" on a string of energy. This was not a metaphorical experience—it was as real an experience as any external experience of a metal rod could be. After mentioning this occurrence to my spiritual teacher, Swami Khecaranatha, he told me of the Tantric

27

practice of the golden rod, wherein as the internal and external breath becomes equalized in rhythm, the kundalini energy may change its state and become stiff as a rod, and the practitioner then may experience the deeper sheaths of the kundalini energy residing within the sushumna.

In these deep states of meditation, accessing the energy of the subtle body is like riding ocean waves that pull one deeper and deeper into a subjective interiority where these entirely real, and yet extremely subtle realms of experience reside. There is no way as of yet to scientifically quantify these experiences, but since the Western perspective has its cultural barometer solidly situated in scientific reality, it is important to assess what current scientific research has been done recently in the field of kundalini that might at least address the material and physiological aspects of kundalini.

Kundalini, Synchronicity, and the New Sciences

Later in his life, Jung not only looked to the past for parallels to his psychological theories but forward to the emerging sciences, particularly physics, to further substantiate and perhaps extend his theories with those of newly developing scientific findings. Jung defined synchronicities as coincidences that "were connected so meaningfully that their 'chance' concurrence would represent a degree of improbability that would have to be expressed by an astronomical figure."[14] These synchronicities correlated an inner, personal experience to an outward, objective incident or phenomena in a way that was significantly meaningful. For instance, you may be thinking of a woman who you haven't spoken to in years, and in that very moment she calls you on the phone. Or you may be thinking of a book you'd like to read, and someone hands you the book the next day without you having mentioned it.

Occurrences of synchronicities are neither random nor arbitrary, and they possess a quality of personal importance for the one experiencing them. These incidences are acausal in nature, having no linear or causal series of linked events that can account for them. By linking external occurrences with the internal subjective realm of emotions and psychological work, Jung was making a connection between spirit and matter, one that suggested a continuum of consciousness. In Goodchild's aforementioned essay, she made the connection between Jung's theory of the synchronicity and the larger field of the subtle body. She suggested that since synchronicity points to an underlying reality beyond the time/space continuum, it "opens us to the subtle body of the world, points us towards evidence of continuing creation based on an acausal foundation, and relies on the co-creative contribution of consciousness through 'meaning' to this on-going creation."[15]

Goodchild correlated similarities between alchemy and synchronicity because both have a relationship of inner experiences and outer events that do not have a perceivable causal trigger. Synchronistic experiences, she noted, have a tendency to result in a "profound shift in attitude resulting from an emotional encounter that opens us to the subtle worlds of the numinous."[16] Such numinous experiences have a possibility of moving us towards individuation or further spiritual growth. In non-dual Tantric philosophy, kundalini is the energy of the individual subtle body, yet it is not considered to be different than the energy of the larger universe. The experience of unity—which in Tantric practices is the direct experience of ourselves as identical with an unbroken continuity of pure consciousness foundational to all manifestation—can be another way of expressing the underlying reality that Jung pointed to in his theory of synchronicity, where internal subjective experience is linked to an external, acausal event.

After Jung's death, the physicist David Bohm in the 1970s developed his theory of what he termed the "holomovement." It was both a theory and response to the generally held mechanistic view of modern and quantum physics that conceived of the universe as consisting of distinct, independent, interacting but ultimately separate elements as the fundamental nature of existence. In contrast to this mechanistic view, Bohm envisioned the holomovement as "the unbroken wholeness of the totality of existence as an undivided flowing movement without borders."[17] In this dynamic environment, the ordered movement of the universe was either explicate or implicate. According to Bohm:

> In terms of the implicate order one may say that everything is enfolded into everything. This contrasts with the explicate order now dominant in physics in which things are unfolded in the sense that each thing lies only in its own particular region of space (and time) and outside the regions belonging to other things.[18]

Bohm did not see the implicate and explicate order as fundamentally separate movements:

> Up till now we have contrasted implicate and explicit orders, treating them as separate and distinct, but the explicit order can be regarded as a particular or distinguished case of a more general set of implicate orders from which the latter can be derived.[19]

Ultimately, Bohm surmised that as the universe was fundamentally whole and unbroken, consciousness could no longer be separated from matter. He wasn't suggesting that a rock and a human have the same degree of consciousness, rather, that consciousness was foundational to the emergence of matter. Here we see the new sciences pointing to what kundalini practitioners directly experienced prior to sophisticated Western scientific discoveries. In Tantra, though there is an infinite array of diversity of manifestation, all manifestation is an expression of an underlying oneness. All the phenomena of the world, from the gross to the subtle, from density to ephemeral thought, are all finite expressions of a foundational and fundamental oneness.

Similarly, Frijof Capra, in explaining the principles underlying organic organizing systems, noted that the mind exists within the body but can perceive externally and receive and process external environmental feedback—and, the same dynamic exists in continually exponential systems. Our minds in our bodies exist within a larger cultural system, which in turn exists within an even larger natural ecosystem. This expansion continues into the planetary and even the universal, cosmic mind. Capra proposed that these intermingling and interacting systems are the self-organizing dynamics of the cosmos.

We might see the compatibility of these scientific findings with that of Tantric and alchemical concepts in which the microcosm (the body) is at core not different than the macrocosm (the world or cosmos). In Tantra, this continuum from pure subtle energy to the grosser forms of matter, including the body, is called *Para-Prakriti*. Para is the name given to the subtlest form of energy, and it is personified as a goddess, Prakriti. Prakriti is the material nature, and yet the materiality is not separate from the subtle energy from which it arose. Bohm's theory of implicate and explicate order and Capra's systems theory wherein individual minds are subsystems of a larger ecological and cosmological mind seem in alignment with Tantric philosophy, a philosophy which is based, as I've explored in Chapter One, on the direct experiences of the practitioners, not only mental constructs.

The relatively new field of neurobiology has added additional perspectives on how kundalini affects the brain and body. Neuroscientist Andrew Newberg noted in his essay in the book *Kundalini Rising*, that during kundalini arousal there are quantitatively measureable changes occurring in the brain. Newberg suggested that the hypothalamus, which regulates and controls several body functions, "including heart rate, blood pressure, and respiration . . . also helps control the autonomic nervous system that regulates our arousal (or sympathetic) and quiescent (parasympathetic functions of the body)." It is this nervous system that seems to play a strong factor in reports of bliss during kundalini processes. For Newburg, "an intriguing aspect of certain mystical experiences is the simultaneous sense of arousal and quiescence. This might be described as an active bliss."[20] Barbara Harris Whitfield in her essay also in the book *Kundalini Rising* described scientific research in which functional magnetic resonance imaging (fMRI), positron-emission computed tomography (PET scans), and single photon emission computed tomography (SPECT), show that the experience of spirituality resides in the limbic system of the brain. It is in this limbic area of the brain that humans feel positive emotions. Whitfield referenced the research of Newburg in which Tibetan Buddhists practicing kundalini meditation were subject to these brain-scanning processes while meditating. When the Buddhists denoted a state of mystical union, the study indicated, "activities of the neocortical brain were functionally cut off from the rest of the brain. At the same time, both the limbic hippocampus and amygdala were more active."[21] In simple terms, the research proves that the psychological states experienced during kundalini and other mystical states do have a physical component as well, bringing mind and body together in a non-dualistic way.

Though these initial findings of the relation between body/mind functioning and kundalini are intriguing and worthy of further pursuit, they are in themselves not a reductive, mechanistic argument for kundalini being "nothing other" than unusual or even pathological functioning of the body. For Newburg, discovering that the brain reacts to kundalini energy does not reduce kundalini merely to a brain function. When the brain was studied while undergoing a kundalini awakening, it was discovered that although certain parts of the brain were more activated, it shouldn't be assumed that kundalini occurred because of a function in the brain. Newburg suggested that it would be just as valid to suggest that the brain was actually responding to the energy of kundalini, participating in the experience rather than creating it. In other words, the brain doesn't "cause" kundalini experiences, but co-participates in the experience with its own corollary response to what's occurring in the subtle body.

The medical doctor and Jungian analyst Lionel Corbett held to a similar perspective. He noted in his book *The Religious Function of the Psyche* that there is no method or scientific measurement that can fundamentally prove the validity of any experience. For example, while doctors may dismiss some ecstatic states as epilepsy, it doesn't diminish that the person experiencing it has a profound experience that might be a window into a transcendent level of consciousness.

I would suggest that science is a valuable and valid perspective that can corroborate and expand knowledge and understanding of experiences of kundalini, but it should not exclude the qualitative research that points beyond the mere materiality or even phenomenology of the experience. Such qualitative research can help us to understand how such experiences affect the total psycho-spiritual facets and positive growth of the individual. Because our culture is thoroughly steeped in the scientific paradigm, research should be inclusive of such perspectives and findings when looking at kundalini from a Western perspective, but in so doing it is important to be wary of the tendency to subtly imply that kundalini becomes legitimized only if it can be quantified by scientific measurement. From a Jungian psychological perspective, kundalini holds legitimacy through its effectiveness in transforming the psychological life of the individual experiencing it, regardless of what brain activity shows up on a medical scan.

The kundalini process may have similar parallels to alchemy and Jung's notion of the continuum of the archetypal forces from the deep, imperceptible layers of the unconscious to the imaginal realms. For example, as kundalini lies dormant, it remains undetected in the body-mind system. But once activated in whatever manner, it reveals all manner of contracted psychic and physical energy, similar to how from a Jungian perspective, archetypal forces control us until they are recognized and integrated into consciousness. These complexes are often heralded by images in dreams, or strong physical or mental affects. Similarly, kundalini, while never visibly seen, makes itself known most obviously through physical symptoms, but this is accompanied by psychological material arising as the chakras are opened, as we'll see most particularly in Jeremy's story in Chapter Seven of this book. Jungians might note these physical affects as indicators of an alchemical transformation of psyche taking place, the spirit in the body stirring awake, or the *mercurius* of Western alchemy moving fluidly through the body-mind system with the goal of creating the philosopher's stone, which is the image of individuation and enlightenment of the individual.

CHAPTER FOUR

East/West Approaches to the Psychology and Philosophy of Kundalini

Jung's seminars on the psychology of kundalini yoga were given in the 1930s, and published as *The Psychology of Kundalini Yoga* in 1996. They were groundbreaking in making connections with and distinctions from Eastern perspectives. They helped to differentiate and define Jung's analytical psychology from Eastern philosophies and other Western psychologies. In light of additional material and scholarly work being done regarding kundalini, as well as the extension and development of Jung's psychology by many scholars and psychologists, it seems valuable to review, and perhaps "re-vision," a Jungian and archetypal psychological perspective of kundalini. In this chapter, I will discuss the key synergistic components Jung felt existed between Eastern thought and his own psychology, as well as noting Jung's sense of the incompatibilities of Eastern thought for the culturally Western mind. I will then discuss two possible approaches to considering kundalini from a Jungian and archetypal psychological perspective, using the concept of Eros consciousness and the myth of Dionysus as guiding principles and images that illustrate particular features of the experiential quality of kundalini in the psyche.

Jung's Western Psychological Perspective on Eastern Philosophy

Much has been written by Jungians on Jung's attitudes towards Eastern philosophies and practices. On the one hand, Jung held a deep interest in Eastern thought, studying Taoism, Buddhism, and Hindu Yoga and

Tantra extensively. He looked to engage Eastern philosophies dialogically, feeling that the wisdom of the East and its focus on realization of the "Self" was similar to his own psychological approach. In addition, Eastern perspectives helped to reinforce and support his theories surrounding his psychology, such as the idea of a larger Self that the individual ego orbited around like a planet to the sun; the notion of the collective unconscious; and the similarities between the concepts of individuation and enlightenment. On the other hand, Jung felt it would be a mistake for Westerners to simply take up the way of the East, believing that it would somehow repress the expression of Western intelligence. Jungian scholar J. J. Clarke, in his book, *Jung and Eastern Thought*, summarized Jung's hesitation for introducing yoga and Tantra as practices for the Westerner—Jung's concern was that Westerners would lose their individual consciousness by totally immersing themselves in the unconscious state. Ultimately such a state of consciousness would mean that Westerners had abandoned their own native way of being in the world, which was heavily weighted toward rational consciousness.

Jung felt that the Eastern psyche had less identification with the ego, and in fact its practices were designed to extinguish the ego altogether. Clarke noted that Jung's understanding was that "yoga prides itself on being able to control even the unconscious processes, so that nothing can happen in the psyche as a whole that is not ruled by a supreme consciousness,"[22] but Jung felt that becoming identified with supreme consciousness would cause Westerners to lose personal objective identification, and become instead identical with the unconscious in a state of what he called *participation mystique*.

In Jung's thinking about Eastern approaches, there is perhaps a conflation of all sects of Hinduism lumped into a whole. For example, in Tantra specifically, there is the concept of *vimarsa*, which is the self-reflective capacity of consciousness. In effect, it is the capacity for consciousness to be aware of itself. Therefore, an immersion into a state of participation mystique, signifying a kind of unconscious absorption with the Self as Jung believed, is not the state of supreme consciousness according to Tantric philosophy. In Tantra, to be in a state of pure consciousness means that such awareness has the discerning capacity to be aware of itself. In their elucidation of the ancient Tantric text, *Tantraloka*, scholars Satya Prakash Singh and Swami Maheshwarananda made a clear distinction between Jung's concept of the collective unconscious and that of the Indian scholar Abinavagupta's conception of the state of *cidakasa,* or space of consciousness. According to Singh and Maheshwar:

> The collective unconscious unfolds itself mainly in a state of deep sleep; cidakasa remains unfolded in all the states of consciousness, however, particularly in the state of samadhi. Collective unconscious is a state of unconsciousness. As distinct from it, cidakasa is actual and real in all the senses of supernal consciousness. It is the realization of the inherent consciousness behind everything.[23]

This offers a counter to Jung's concern that Westerners would simply become absorbed in an unconscious state with no sense of individual identity if they were to attempt deep states of meditation.

The scholar Patrick Mahaffey noted in his essay "Self-Inquiry in C. G. Jung's Depth Psychology and Hindu Yoga Traditions," that Tantric Shaivism has many meditation techniques aimed at assisting the practitioner to hone a state of *samadhi,* or union with all, without needing to go into a state of introverted meditation. Mahaffey pointed to the Sanskrit terms *atma-vyapti,* referring to the inward process of experiencing unity with the self, and *shiva-vyapti,* which is experiencing or becoming one with the world. Shiva-vyapti is the state of complete liberation, where a person is "free to creatively express the physical, emotional, and mental powers of his or her being in the world for the good of all."[24] Therefore, according to Tantra, there is no need to remove oneself from the world, or go into a trance-like state, never to return to waking consciousness.

Even though Jung misunderstood this aspect of the Eastern tradition, it seems Tantra is even more compatible with Jung's psychology than he thought, in that it emphasizes worldly engagement as much as it does internal meditation. J. J. Clarke summarized the essential points of Tantra that drew Jung into intellectual engagement with it:

> First, a dynamic, developmental view of the personality, with a strong teleological tendency towards self-fulfillment; thus, the chakras are not only centers of growth, but can be viewed as stages of development, symbolized by the ascent of the kundalini. Secondly, a holistic outlook which draws no absolute distinction between psychic and somatic

factors; thus the psyche is not a disembodied entity but is mapped onto the body's inner topography. Thirdly, a positive, life-affirming view of the body, the passions, and the shadowy regions of the psyche . . . . Fourthly, a symbolic system which employs complex images rather than words to express psychic processes, and which encourages us to view the psyche as a meaningful structure.[25]

Mahaffey also felt the affinities between Jung's approach and the Tantric one when he suggested that had Jung "allowed for the possibility that the awakening process is an important and viable endeavor for everyone, not just for Eastern practitioners, the ground for investigating the complementarity of the two processes could have been established."[26] Eastern practices have gained solid footing in the West, and it doesn't seem to have created negative cultural or psychological results thus far.

Kundalini, Anima, and Eros

Kundalini, often depicted in Tantra iconography as a goddess, is considered the individual expression of Shakti, the divine feminine force of manifestation. From a Jungian perspective, kundalini as psychological symbol might be conceived as an *anima* image. In Jung's psychological use of the term, he called the anima the projection-making factor in man, and though usually relegated to the unconscious, this image appears in dreams, and fantasies in a physical form. According to Jung, men possess an anima image and the corresponding psychic image for a woman he called the *animus*. This inner image, which Jung called the "soul-image" for either a man or woman, represents an inner stance that is unconscious and contrary to his or her persona or conscious attitude in life. While Jung's notion seems antiquated in light of the evolution of the more gender fluid continuum that is acknowledged today, the notion that there is an inner anima and anima in every individual that juxtaposes the external gender identity still holds some validity as is evidenced in dreams and even external projection such as romantic projections on an "other."

In Tantra, kundalini is a feminine principle that lies within men and women equally—it is like a movement of higher consciousness that reveals unconscious hidden patterns, rather than a gendered image in the psyche. James Hillman, in his work, *Anima: An Anatomy of a Personified*

Notion, is in closer alignment with the Tantric view, when he stated, "We can hardly attribute anima to the male sex only. The 'feminine' and 'life' as well as the Chinese, Indian, and Gnostic analogies to anima are relevant to men and women equally."[27]

But along with a gendered notion of anima and animus, Jung also believed that the anima was the archetype of meaning itself. In Jung's view the voluntary surrender of personal will, which would be a defeat for the ego, was an invaluable step in personal and spiritual development, for when the ego was stilled, the anima, the archetype of meaning according to Jung, could emerge. In this sense we can imagine equivalences in tone and resonance with the symbolic and lived experience of kundalini, which is considered the foundational force of all manifestation, the energy behind the creation of all life, and also it often requires a stilling of our own personal will, or on occasion may emerge when our egoic stance is involuntarily renounced, as may be the case in moments of trauma.

Another concept of Jung's that is relevant to connecting Eastern and Western approaches to the psyche is his notion of the *syzygy*, which referred to any instance of a pair of opposites, whether they were in alignment or in opposition. Syzygy is closer to the notion of the ida and pingala energy channels in the kundalini energy structure, the feminine and masculine energies that meet at each chakra center. According to Tantra, it is the resolution of these opposite energies within the sushumna, the central energy channel in the body, in which unity of consciousness occurs. Tantric scholars Satya Prakash Singh and Swami Maheshvarananda, referring to the Tantric text of the *Tantra Loka*, which is the foundational text of Tantra, noted that Jung's discovery of the male and female elements in the psyche was anticipated by the foremost scholar and kundalini master, Abhinavagupta, who elaborated on the concept of the *androgyne*, an image that is depicted as both Shiva and Shakti, a hermaphrodite. They noted that Abhinavagupta's commentary "has a long history behind it anticipated by thousands of years as its roots lie in the Brhadaranyaka Upanishad."[28] Similarly, Lilian Silburn said:

> The representation of S[h]iva as a hermaphrodite, *ardha-vira*, is a favorite one in Indian iconography, the right side of the body being masculine and the left, feminine. Thereby is expressed in a concrete form the free, independent divine energy, as the presences of both sexes

in a single body reconstitutes the original oneness of the opposite principles dividing the universe.[29]

James Hillman, in his psychological commentary on the kundalini experience of Gopi Krishna, also suggested that as a shift from the pingala (masculine) energy channel moves to the ida (feminine) energy channel occurs, there is a shift and activation of the unconscious feminine side of the personal psyche. He also asserted that this shakti-kundalini is not made to be of service or support to the masculine energy, but rather that the feminine energy or anima has its own expression and activity, and in any person, male or female, the feminine force or anima must have its own channel of activity. Human beings are only a channel through which this energy expresses itself.

In Tantric practice, although the image of kundalini is depicted as feminine, ultimately gender is not relevant, as kundalini is a latent force within all human beings. However, if kundalini is considered as an energy that has a particular quality of consciousness, it could be said that it is the feminine aspect of Eros, rather than masculine aspect of Logos, that characterizes the kundalini experience and process, and even indicates the direction of psychological transformation. Jung held a theoretical concept that the inner masculine image of animus was associated with Logos, an archetype of knowledge and rationality, while Eros depicted a more feminine consciousness that possessed qualities of connection, relationship, and love. If we remove the categorization of which gender has a dominant propensity for either kind of quality of consciousness, then we may suggest that Eros is the relational, creative, perhaps more intuitive form of consciousness closely aligned with direct forms of knowing and experiential wisdom. Phenomenologically, as kundalini awakens, it unveils this quality of direct insight and knowledge. This direct experience often brings with it a sense of wonder, compassion, bliss, and love, which is then outwardly directed and expressed in relationship to others, increasing our connection with and our sense of well-being in the outer world. Von Franz, in her work *Reflections of the Soul*, spoke of Eros and love as a supreme activator of psychological transformation.

Love is such a fateful factor in the life of every human being because, more than anything else, it has the power to release the living from their ego-bound consciousness; it brings us a hint of a transcendental happening, making it possible for us to attend a divine play of the union of Shiva and Shakti, god and goddess, beyond the banality of this earthly life.[30]

In this sense, Eros is earthly and transcendent, moving within and yet beyond the physically manifest realm. John Weir Perry, in his book *Trials of the Visionary Mind: Spiritual Emergency and the Renewal Process*, noted after years of working with patients going through psychologically challenging processes that would normally be labeled as psychotic, that with compassionate interaction, these people often had positive outcomes. For Perry, compassion and love were the ultimate goal of the whole individual. This wholeness was not an intellectual understanding but a directly experienced sense of oneness with all beings. Such experiences led to more intimacy in relationships and the actual experience of oneness, not just a belief in the concept of oneness.

Perry also noted that there were larger cultural implications to this movement of psyche into a more relational mode. He suggested that an Eros approach to the world rather than a Logos approach, which often brings with it desire for power and domination, "operates according to the receptive, a principle that motivates us to open ourselves fully to the nature and needs of the world around us."[31]

Culturally and philosophically speaking, Tantra was similarly an Eros approach in Hinduism that emerged as a response to the more patriarchal, socially elite, and orthodox Vedic philosophy. Scholar and spiritual teacher Swami Shankarananda, in his book *The Yoga of Kashmir Shaivism,* compared the oppositional approaches of Veda and Tantra to the traditional and philosophic art forms in the West:

> Just as in Western art there seems an eternal polarity between the classical and the romantic sensibilities, or in Nietzsche's terms, the Apollonian and Dionysian, so too, Indian spirituality has its own polarity: Veda and Tantra. Perhaps these two represent two chambers of the human heart or the two hemispheres of the human brain.[32]

According to Shankarananda, the Vedantic perspective and teaching was one of knowledge and detachment. The forms of the world were considered less real than the inner experience of the Self, where Self is defined as pure consciousness. Pure consciousness in this sense is similar to Jung's own notion of the Self as the totality of consciousness. For Vedics, by using a process of discrimination, one could negate the relative reality of the world and come to the direct experience of the supreme Self.

Whereas Shankarananda describes the Vedic philosophy in masculine, fatherly terms, he viewed Tantra as the archetypally feminine spirituality of the mother. Tantra developed as both a devotional practice and a practical methodology for enlightenment, one that allowed for full participation in the world. "Where the Vedic path . . . called for renunciation and control of the desire nature, Tantra . . . sought to sublimate and redirect existing impulses and energies, not suppress them. For the Tantric, the world was not the enemy but the embodiment of God."[33] Devotees of Tantra worshipped female divinities and believed that enlightenment could be attained by engaging the powerful energy of kundalini, cultivating profound insights and awareness attained with its arousal and subsequent progression through the chakras. Tantra challenged the traditional social structures of the time, including allowing women and people of all classes to participate in esoteric and highly secret practices normally kept hidden from anyone but high priests and scholars.

In Tantric philosophy, Shakti, as the cosmic aspect of the individual kundalini, is considered the source behind the appearance and experience of all polarities. It is the totality of the manifest world in its myriad diverse forms, and it evolves and emerges as a result of the union of opposites. The tension of the oppositional polarity is resolved in a union that is expressed and felt as bliss, as love, and as creative expression. Shakti-Kundalini also acts as the instigator of the integration of masculine and feminine energies within the individual, and those energies might be more aligned with the Jungian sense of the anima and animus, though in Tantra, each individual contains both. Kundalini, then, from a Jungian perspective, might be conceptualized as the Eros aspect of consciousness; it's the force that assists in integrating oppositional complexes in the psyche and fostering a relational dynamic between the feminine and masculine principles.

Kundalini as a Dionysian Movement of Psyche

As Shankarananda noted, the activation and progression of kundalini in the psyche is more closely associated with a Dionysian movement than an Apollonian one. Archetypally Dionysus's domain is that of the emotions—particularly the instinctive or suppressed ones—as well as women, wine, madness, and tragedy. I've explored the ways in which kundalini is connected to Eros consciousness, which has been historically associated with women and the feminine. Dionysus is also associated with women and Eros consciousness. But it is particularly Dionysus's association with divine madness that I wish to explore further in this section, as it relates to kundalini and extends to experiences of "spiritual madness" often associated with the kundalini process.

Both the Dionysus movement of the psyche and the kundalini process are grounded in the body, and both have associations with the feminine. It was women, called the Maenads, who made up the cult of worshippers of Dionysus, and their worship included ritualistic, ecstatic dancing. This embodied behavior could bring worshippers to ecstasy or tragedy, as exemplified in the story of the Bacchae when Pentheus' own mother and aunts, who were maddened with divine ecstasy, ripped him apart. There is an element of necessary repression that accompanies the Dionysian impulse in the psyche, one that allows for the instinctive element to surface and move beyond socially constrictive norms, but one that, by its very instinctive nature, can be dangerous if it is not somewhat contained. Thus the Dionysian movement of psyche holds the polarity of both ecstasy and tragedy in a dynamic tension.

In our current more Apollonian-weighted Western culture, this innate urge of the psyche is further repressed, and arguably when such urges do erupt, they lack the context and framework that allows for the energy to be channeled in a positive and transformative direction, often exhibiting more hedonistic, shallow behavior that corrodes rather than nourishes the psyche. Kundalini is a similar impulse arising in the psyche, but I would say that it is the repression of the energy coupled with lack of understanding in both the individual and in the general Western culture that may result in a madness that appears more like a psychotic break than a divine ecstasy. The Jungian psychiatrist John Weir Perry worked with many patients undergoing psychotic episodes, many of whom came through the episode and moved over time to a fuller and more whole sense of self. For Perry, it became clear that labeling a client as psychotic had more to do with the judgment society had for spates of the non-rational. When such an individual was treated with kindness and patience, and the labels of insanity were removed, he witnessed many clients organically going into remission, or returning to a more balanced mental state.

Many adepts of kundalini emphasize the benefits of having a teacher to guide one through the process, specifically because the movement of kundalini through the body-mind system can be so utterly outside of cultural norms, and because the movement unearths and restructures the psyche, beyond the conscious will or wishes of the individual. It is the contextualization and normalization the teacher can give the student that allows the energy of kundalini to move through the entire psychic system—yet even with a teacher, the kundalini process is not without its trials. James Hillman, in referencing not only Gopi Krishna's radical kundalini awakening, but addressing any person going through profound transformational shifts, underscores the critical importance of an objective witness to provide the person with psychological knowledge as well as confirmation that other people have gone through similar processes. Knowing one is not alone and that there is a purpose and aim of deepening personal development and insight can go a long way in helping people open into the process with curiosity rather than with fear, which is at its heart what this book is all about.

Perhaps Jung, in his own confrontation with the unconscious, would have benefited from such a person, as alienation can compound the psychological difficulties. Most likely, Jung did talk to people about the eruption of the unconscious into his conscious awareness, and in fact did find some solace speaking to an Indian yogi; however, he may not have felt supported in his crisis by the overall culture surrounding him. Perhaps Jung experienced a kundalini awakening that he largely processed on his own through both his intellectual acuity and his technique he called active imagination, as well as his art-making that can be seen in *The Red Book*. In other individuals with similarly challenging psychological material erupting, Perry noted that people going through episodes of psychosis go through a kind or psychic reorganization, in which old assumptions and beliefs disintegrate and emerge with a new inner understanding of themselves, society, and the larger world.

Though Perry is referring to temporarily psychotic individuals, and one can see similarities in extreme kundalini processes, I would not wish to overly conflate the two psychic states. Kundalini is not psychosis—though for people who are unprepared or unable to cope or regulate the process, it may feel like a psychotic episode and as a result, potentially lead to an experience of psychosis. In my personal experience working with kundalini energy for almost 30 years, kundalini has a tendency to self-regulate. By this I mean that when the energy is particularly intense, it seems to have a rhythm that naturally abates when a particular level of understanding or consciousness has been achieved. Medical doctor Lee Sannella noted that kundalini "symptoms" tend to diminish over time, which corroborates my experience. According to Sannella, since the kundalini process is one of purifying the body-mind system, and the person is a limited system, the kundalini process is also self-limiting. The turbulence that occurs in the body-mind system along the way is then actually therapeutic insofar as it removes the tensions and conflicts that could lead to pathology.

In this way, much like the psyche's tendency to move towards wholeness as Jung suggested, kundalini moves the psycho-spiritual process towards wholeness and completion with periods of intensity and periods of relative calm in a cycle that is somewhat predicated on the individual's engagement and focus on the process. Just as when we pay attention to our dreams the psyche seems to respond by supplying richer and more constant images, so focusing and being open to the process of kundalini fosters a more profound, full movement of the energy. Similar to Sannella, transpersonal psychologist Roberto Assagioli made a clear distinction between regressive and progressive affects and symptoms in individuals going through psychological challenges. According to Assagioli:

> The neuro-psychological symptoms of ordinary patients are usually regressive in nature. These patients have been unable to form the necessary internal and external frameworks contributing to the normal development of personality. . . . The ills produced by the travail of spiritual development are clearly progressive in nature. . . . They are by-products of temporary conflicts and imbalances between the conscious personality and the spiritual energies bursting through. . . . A cure that is appropriate for a patient in the first group [regressive] is inadequate for, and may even be harmful to, an individual in the second [progressive].[34]

Like the Dionysian movement within the psyche, temporary horrors, instinctual urges, and breaks with culturally sanctioned behaviors are part of the deepening and growth of individuals, connecting them to their own spiritual essence and soul. In The *Myth of Analysis,* James Hillman suggested that re-engagement of the culturally repressed Dionysian consciousness means to embrace our psychological bisexuality, by which he was implying that it is not only the masculine and Logos-oriented consciousness that should be acknowledged, but also the feminine Eros consciousness. According to Hillman, when both the male and females aspects are conjoined, it is an integrative gesture of the active and receptive principles, and also of the cycle of life and death. The Dionysian energy arises and subsides in a cyclic process, and this process may occur many times throughout an individual's life. Hillman also contended that experiencing Dionysian consciousness cannot be a willful act—which would suppose an Apollonic movement of consciousness trying to impose or create a particular experience—but rather, that the insight and depth that results from an influx of Dionysian energy happens of its own accord and its own intelligence.

Hillman's bisexuality metaphor also points to the importance of the body in psychological and spiritual transformation. In his commentary on Gopi Krishna, Hillman pointed out that, much like Krishna himself, it would behoove us to understand that deep transformation of consciousness doesn't leave the body behind. The body changes and accommodates new consciousness as a woman's body accommodates and changes when life grows inside her. These changes may be unnerving, but they are a natural process in the progression of consciousness. Dionysian consciousness, as well as the kundalini process, includes the body as well as the mind. The kundalini process, with its integration of masculine and feminine energies, its Eros-oriented way of knowing, its manner of seemingly entering and erupting within the internal awareness of the individual without conscious consent, and finally its tendency to bring about the death of calcified patterns in the psyche, can be viewed from a Jungian and archetypal perspective as an erotic Dionysian movement of psyche originating in the Self. The purpose of this movement is the urge towards psychic wholeness—whether that wholeness is termed individuation or enlightenment.

In the above sections, I've explored how the kundalini process may result in "symptoms" similar to those considered pathological in a Western cultural construct, but may ultimately lead to psychic transformation, especially when placed in cultural and historical context. It is also relevant to consider how external trauma may be a factor in instigating a kundalini process. Jungian analyst Donald Kalsched, an expert in working with trauma patients from a Jungian perspective, explained that many people who have survived trauma, whether sustained in early childhood trauma or in a specific traumatic event, "often have a deep understanding of a sacred world that sustains them, even in the most depriving and abusive of human environments." For Kalsched, acknowledging this sacred or spiritual world as real, even if "recruited for defensive purposes," does not imply that those experiences or worlds are simply fantasies of the imagination to defend against the trauma, but rather a digging deep into internal resources that are tapped as a result of external difficulty. Kalsched remarked, "There are also few, if any, atheists among trauma survivors."[35] This may be akin to accessing the deeper, instinctive aspects of Dionysian consciousness normally dormant or suppressed by the ordinary ego consciousness.

Medical doctor and researcher Yvonne Kason, in her exploration of near death experiences (NDEs) observed that people who had NDEs early in life had a higher percentage of later kundalini experiences. Such a connection indicates that once an individual has traversed the pathways to these deeper elements and energies of the psyche, those pathways and places are more easily accessed in subsequent periods of life; perhaps once seen, they cannot be unseen. This also harkens back to Jung's death/rebirth archetype and Hillman's connection of this archetype to Dionysian consciousness. The ego consciousness both in near-death experiences and kundalini experiences is forced to relinquish its dominant position, if only temporarily, and in so doing, other types or layers of consciousness can move to the forefront, revealing a fuller depth of psychic life. For Hillman, engaging in Dionysian consciousness and loosening the knot of a singularly Apollonian consciousness means transforming consciousness through the feminine. Metaphorical bisexuality is balanced between the feminine and masculine modes of consciousness, and therefore the feminine is understood as a valuable and necessary aspect of the psyche as a whole. Hillman believed that in order to access a more complete consciousness, we must commit to reinvestment in the feminine aspects of psyche available to all of us. I suggest the individuals undergoing a kundalini process are engaging in this feminine mode of consciousness, allowing this energy to work through them for deep psychic transformation and integration.

PART TWO

Kundalini Stories

"There is no greater agony than bearing an untold story inside you."
Maya Angelou

In the following pages you'll read the stories of five people—Ryan, Colleen, Jeremy, Maria, and me—who experienced and continue to experience kundalini. These stories are not the whole story; kundalini can weave its presence and power throughout a person's lifetime. But they're stories that profoundly touched the teller. You'll read of unusual experiences in meditation, experiences that happened during normal waking life, and experiences during those nocturnal hours where the landscape of dream is dominant.

The telling of these stories had powerful and transformative effects on all of us. It's not easy speaking about unusual occurrences that herald a kundalini experience. It's an act of courage to give voice to experiences that might label one as crazy. For some of us, the events leading up to our kundalini awakening were traumatic. For others, the telling of the story impacted our dreams, lead to spontaneous synchronicities, and revealed sudden insight.

There is power in the stories that lie inside us, and when they are allowed their narrative space, they change the teller and the witness. It was my intention to focus on the heart of the story and their images, in the timber and tone of the words that coax the soul of these profound and often touching experiences of kundalini out of their hiding place to shine with their inner effulgence. I hope you'll feel connected to these stories and they have a positive transformational effect for you as well.

You'll notice that these stories are not told just in words. They're also told in physical movement and in art, in journal writing and dream recording. In 2017, each person met with me in person three times, over three months, in order to track the shifts in the psyche that occurred as a result of our time together. The majority of the participants are meditation practitioners in my spiritual community, but I did not know all of them well when we started working together. I met one participant, Colleen, during my time as an expat in Indonesia. My focus in my interview process with all of them was on how these kundalini experiences changed their perspective as well as their action/s or relationship to the world, as I knew it had changed mine. I was also curious if the traditional, primarily Eastern imagery of kundalini, such as the snake, the goddess, and the caduceus, necessarily accompanied a Westerner undergoing a kundalini activation. If symbols arose that were different, what could be understood of them from a depth psychological perspective?

The Jungian analyst and scholar Joan Chodorow noted that Jung often suggested that the images his patients generated in their sessions were to be lived with and related to for some period of time, and this is what I asked of my participants and myself. Each participant worked with drawings they made during the interview sessions. They took their images home, spent time journaling about them in active imagination or even movement dialogues. They recorded their dreams in the time between our sessions, and noted any significant shifts.

Along with interview questions, I used a movement-based, somatic, expressive arts technique called the "psychokinetic imagery process," based on the work of Anna and Daria Halprin, co-founders of the Tamalpa Institute. The psychokinetic imagery process is very similar to Jung's conception and practice of active imagination. It involves using the body in dialogue with emerging sensations and images in a dialectical manner that reveals deep realms and resources in the psyche, beyond the ego or rational consciousness structures we normally engage. This technique utilizes movement, drawing, and creative journaling and dialogue in an interactive, iterative manner in which every mode of expression informs every other. For instance, we might begin with a sensation we identify in our body, and then that sensation is given expression in a movement or series of movements. This movement is informed somatically—that is, it comes from the internal experience of the mover, not from an external idea of how the movement should be expressed. The next step may be to take the movement experience and represent it in a drawing. The images need not be a literal representation or "artistic" in any way. The drawings are a visual resonance of the experience of the movement. From either movement or drawing, insights might develop. One can "move" a drawing using a shape, color, or other aspect of the drawing to inspire a further exploration. A poetic, written, or verbal expression may add a contextual framework and understanding of the entire exploration.

I encourage you, dear reader, to also keep a journal while reading these stories. You might keep track of your dreams, become aware of a sudden spate of synchronicities, or feel other shifts in your body-mind system. In this way you will participate even more deeply with these stories and perhaps have your own insights and connections along the way.

CHAPTER FIVE

Ryan's Story: Integrating the Images and Energy of Cobra and Monk

Ryan is a soft-spoken, tall, slender artist and poet in his early 30s. He sports several tattoos and was part of the hardcore punk and graffiti scene in his teenage years and early 20s in the Seattle area. For Ryan, hardcore punk was not about violence or aggression, but rather about engagement and activism. Ryan explained to me in an email during our work together that, "despite the old cliché of it being 'more than music' for me it really was. So much of how I view myself and the world came from my involvement in a community that presented challenging information and ideas in a way that was energized but accepting. As aggressive as the music is, I also wish to emphasize how anti-violent the scene in the Pacific Northwest was." If there was violence in the community or at events, it would make it much more difficult to find venues where the music could be performed and the community could gather.

Ryan also found support for his life choices in this community. He shared, "Coming from a household ravaged by addiction I had decided very early in life not to drink or do drugs. In hardcore I found a Straight Edge community with these same values to support me in this choice. Additionally, I learned through zines and bands about factory farming, the animal rights movement, and many social and political injustices both foreign and domestic that I had not previously encountered in my public education." Through the Straight Edge community, he became a vegan, a diet he continues to adhere to. Ryan also felt that same kind of vibe with graffiti groups. His email continued, "Graffiti, like hardcore, shared this [do it yourself] spirit (although certainly not ringing of the same 'drug free' manifestos) of being available and achievable to anyone. Kids growing up where I did didn't dream of becoming a Picasso-like figure to be hung in the Louvre someday with works sold for millions. This was unfathomable; but expression, creativity, and freedom as tangible realities within these more approachable avenues were wholly attainable to even the lowest among us and it is there where these counter cultures best serve and truly succeed."

Ryan and I met through our spiritual practice and were friendly acquaintances, but we didn't know each other well. I sensed, prior to knowing anything about his participation in the hardcore punk and graffiti scenes, that underneath Ryan's unassuming and sensitive demeanor there was a rebel. Ryan struck me as a keen observer of people and situations, with an insightful but also wary eye to the world around him. I got to know Ryan a little better during a six-week spiritual retreat in India. Still, there seemed much of Ryan that he kept to himself.

The First Interview

To begin our first interview together, I asked Ryan to describe a kundalini experience he was currently having or had in the past. Ryan told me that prior to the experience in Ganeshpuri, he did not really connect to the word "kundalini." He enjoyed his meditation practice and felt subtle shifts within it, but he hadn't experienced such a strong visceral sense of energy since his experience in India.

"As soon as I closed my eyes I saw a cobra," Ryan told me. Describing the image of the cobra, he said, "It was almost as if you were standing in a room and you can't see behind you, but you know, 'Oh, so-and-so is right there, oh, there's a cobra right there.'" Ryan could see the outline of it, "almost like it was carved on something." As he talked about the cobra image, his chest expanded and his hands gestured from his heart outwards. Ryan shared that he stayed present and open to the image as our mutual spiritual teacher Nathaji came to give him shakti transmission through touch. Ryan described the touch as the "normal thing" except for at the end, when it felt like Nathaji "was yanking a fish out of water" from his heart. Then the energy really started moving.

"I just remember all of this energy coming down, so much so that it weighed my body down to the point that I was still trying to sit in meditation posture but I couldn't hold my upper half up because it just felt like this really subtle but really dense stuff was coming in. And then I started getting all this really intense pranic breath that I didn't even know what it was. At that point, my body was just doing things and I was being aware of it, and aware that I was kind of in control of it, and also that I shouldn't try to control it—I should just say, 'Okay, this is really intense, but it's not dangerous and it's not scary, and I should just keep my hands off it and let it happen.'"

The experience continued to unfold with more pranic breathing, and then Ryan explained, "I started to feel this electrical pulse and current, and it just felt like every nadi[i] and every channel was moving, was pulsating. I remember, I just kept trying to sit and hold the mudra, and I could feel energy moving everywhere, but for some reason, it felt like every channel spun around the mudra, and so, to hold it, I was almost trembling, as if you were trying to hold onto something. I was really, really jolted. It almost felt a little bit like being electrocuted. . . I remember lying down in child's pose and crying really strongly and not with any emotional content, really, but just something had to go, and it was almost like crying was the release."

He continued, "So that went on for a long time, and intermittently through that, I would get the surge again. At one point, I guess it would be like a kriya[ii], but I was in child's pose and then my arms went up in the air and I went up on the crown of my head and I could feel all this energy coming up from the ground through my head."

Ryan felt like both the crying and the energy seemed to happen without any volition on his part. After the class, there was a break before returning to the question and answer portion of the class. Ryan had gone to his room to compose himself but then realized he was running late so he began to run back to class. As he was running to be on time, "I ran face-to-face with Nathaji as he was walking in, and I just remember locking eyes with him and looking at his face and just love pouring out from his face, and then I just cried again. I guess that's the best way I can

---

[i] In yoga, a nadi is a point or channel of energy, and a mudra is a particular position of the body, usually the hands.

[ii] In yoga traditions, and particularly with kundalini practices, a kriya is a movement of the body when the energy of kundalini runs through it. The energy encounters a denser, contracted energy, and as it pushes through or unblocks the contracted energy, there is often an experience of a jolting, and the body may respond in various, spontaneous movements as a result.

explain it. Up to that point, I felt like I was getting tremendous benefit from class and I was growing and I was getting more still inside and my meditations were getting better, but I had never felt energy like that. I'd had really subtle physical sensations, but nothing like that. That, to me, stands out, and after doing this for a couple years, it's one of the most powerful representations of what kundalini can do."

I asked Ryan how the experience impacted him in the days and even months after it occurred. Ryan replied, "It felt like the days following maybe brought things up. I can remember working through some stuff." We explored together what this "stuff" consisted of. Ryan explained that prior to this experience he was having doubts about his place in the practice. He didn't question the validity of the practice, the philosophy, or the teacher, but rather he was inquiring of himself if it was the right fit for him. Interestingly, after the experience happened, those questions increased rather than decreased. Ryan described the emotional tension of that inquiry as even being "torturous." Ryan's partner, who was also on the retreat, suggested that this concern around belonging might have deeper roots to explore.

Opening seriously to the possibility of a deeper issue trying to surface, Ryan sat with the feeling of doubt, and, he shared, "What started to emerge from me was mistrust and this feeling that I can't trust that this is going to get me what I need or what I want." After working with this issue somatically and with quite a bit of emotional charge, Ryan felt a particular narrative arise. "This narrative started to progress of seeing this monk sitting in a stone temple or a stone cave, and I could feel him—I could feel his body and I felt like that was me. I remember sitting and the more I stayed with him, the more I felt like I could feel myself in him, my characteristics. I felt him sitting on this rock or on this mountain and then I felt him die, and it felt like he had some heart failure."

He continued, "I was sitting trying to contact this memory or even, if it's not a memory, whatever it was, I could really feel it happening in my body in a subtle way. Even sitting as him and trying to feel his image, I could feel these sensations in my body that I don't usually feel. It almost felt like I had more energy when I was trying to contact that memory, or trying to sit as him. Basically, I felt him die and the next thing I remember is this sense that, 'Okay, I've done all this work and now I've died and I'm going to just let go and everything's going to change.' And the next thing I remember is the hand of God grabbing my little soul and throwing me back down into manifestation and separation and confusion and pain and misery, and it feels like that touches on my issue that I don't trust God, or that I don't trust that I could do all this work and it could get me anywhere. That mistrust seemed, to me, to be the bigger issue, not Nathaji says this that I don't understand or agree with, therefore I shouldn't be in this practice. It's this fear that I'm going to align with the losing party or I'm going to make all my best effort and it's not going to work, it's not going to get me where I'm hoping to go. That was a pretty big shift and a pretty big thing to come out and to work with and to try to let go of."

While Ryan shared his story, his body movements contracted. His chest caved in, and his hands gestured inward and curled at his heart, almost like how mummies are found curled inwards in their tombs. Even the atmosphere in the room seemed to change, getting heavier and more still, as if a low-pressure system had entered the room and the barometer had dropped significantly.

Ryan allowed himself to remain open to various possibilities as to whether his experience was a memory (from this life or another), or a narrative that gave form to a deep-seated feeling. What seemed most important in the moment were the feelings of anguish, sadness, betrayal, and mistrust that created a barrier to a sense of belonging in his spiritual community, and also his connection to a larger sense of divinity or sacredness for himself. Ryan felt that just allowing those feelings to arise and flow through him took a lot of the charge out of them and eased the intensity of questioning his place in the practice. He noticed that a lot of "smaller feelings that were springing up from it" had dissipated. Yet he did not think this monk image and some of the feelings were completely resolved.

After this discussion, it seemed an appropriate time to focus on bringing the strong images that Ryan talked about into the body. Starting with the image of the cobra, I asked him to feel where the sense of cobra was in his body. Although fighting some self-consciousness about moving in front of me, he noticed that he felt an elongation of his spine. As he spoke I noticed that his arms and hands were also doing an opening gesture in front of his chest. Bringing his attention to this gesture, he reported that the experience felt really open, and in staying with the movement for a while he felt "more strength or more presence" when his spine was straight. He also reported that the cobra image in him felt as if it were "installed," in the sense that it was permanent and that he only had to tune into his body to experience the cobra's presence.

I asked him to draw the image from this felt sense of the cobra. I gave him about ten minutes to draw, telling him to take less time or more as he needed. Below is the image Ryan drew.

Cobra

The images are of three separate cobra shapes: the far left image is in purple, the middle image is blue, and the lower right image is green. There are two thick lines: the upper line is red and the lower line below the middle cobra is yellow. We both took some time staying present to the image and noticing what was intriguing and compelling, and what thoughts arose from witnessing the image. I mentioned that the purple and blue colors were striking to me. Ryan responded by saying he didn't usually see anything during meditation, "but one of the only times that's happened is the first time I came to class with Nathaji, and I saw blue, purple, and then a white, almost clear color. I had my eyes closed and it filled my vision, it was almost interacting, the purple and the blue and the clear were mixing together. As I look at it now, I notice the dark purple or the dark blue and the white, clear. Just looking at that now reminded me of that."

I mentioned to him that I was also curious about the green shape, and that it reminded me of a bowl or a well.

"It almost feels like that's the heart that was holding all these things. I don't know, like they came from that opening or they moved through that," Ryan said. I mentioned also that there was a strong red line and strong movement toward the line, almost like I could hear a whooshing sound as it moved to the right and upwards.

"Yeah, and as you mentioned it too, a lot of the lines have this, or at least the way I drew them as an ascension, or moving forward and up." He also liked the sense of movement; even though it was not a literal rendering of the experience and image, the movement captured how the experience felt in his body. I ask him if the picture had a name, what would it be? He named it "Cobra."

Ryan then worked with the image of the monk. He sat with a sense of the image in his body. He sank further back into his seat, head slightly bowed. He said that the image was very heavy in his body, almost like wanting to curl up and collapse, "like when an animal curls up in a storm." I asked him to render a drawing of the monk, to bring him visually into the room. This is what emerged.

Monk

We both noticed that there was a lot of activity around the head, with a kind of black halo and black lines by the lower body. There is yellow emanating out of the face and towards the back of the halo, and the black lines at the left and right sides of the body also have a dark purple color shooting through them. The body remained largely unformed and empty. Ryan noticed that even though the picture was mostly in black and grey, there was some light around the head, like "sunlight emanating." For Ryan, even though it felt like there was a lot of "dark, tumultuousness," there was also a "glimmer or sunlight."

I pointed out that the purple was an intriguing color in the picture. Ryan said, "I think that purple, and especially that color, to me, has a spiritual feel." I asked him to do some movement with the image, and to also go back and forth between the cobra and the monk image and see where they were in his body. Ryan was surprised to discover that the cobra was very much at the top of his head and around his heart, while the monk image was in his lower body, like a big boulder sitting in his second chakra and lower back area. He remarked while continuing to move, "It's interesting, because it feels really dead in my lower body, but it still feels pretty alive in the space around my head and my heart." There was a sense that when he contacted Cobra in his body, he wanted to move, and when he contacted Monk, he wanted to sit down.

Going back and forth in movement dialogue with the images, gradually there was a movement in his entire body—his weight shifting from leg to leg and his hands beginning to open and close as if tentatively experimenting with curling up and then opening in a small, safe movement. Watching Ryan was like witnessing a moving meditation. He was genuinely surprised and intrigued to find these images so concretely located in different areas of his body. As he continued to move the different images, Ryan noticed that the images were separate, like the cobra was stacked on top of the image of the monk—and as he described it, I had a flash of an image of Ryan's body holding within it a totem consisting of both the chakras and the images of Monk and Cobra, separate but of one body. Ryan further noted that these images and energies were not "necessarily trying to get away from each other, but it's almost like oil and water. They separate, even if they're put together."

As the movement exploration came to an end, Ryan had one last insight that the two images seemed to represent "two things that maybe haven't quite merged or unified or integrated yet. Or they're two things that are operating separately that don't need to. So in a way, that's what I get, is this sense from both that they could come together, or that integration could occur and that instead of feeling them as two such different things, there's room for it to overlap more."

The Second Interview

The first thing I noticed about Ryan as he entered my office was that he appeared confident and relaxed, with a sense of strong presence I hadn't noticed in our first interview. His blue eyes were focused and direct when talking with me, and his entire being emanated vividness, almost like his physical body had been colored in. I felt relaxed myself and noticed a feeling of anticipation at hearing how his explorations and experiences had unfolded over the past month.

Ryan settled into his seat and began by sharing that he had put the images up above his desk and noticed that he was often drawn to look at them, like a magnetic force drawing him into his office so that he could be in their presence. He noticed that, over time, when he would go to sit with the images, an interesting thing began to take place—an integration of the image and the movement that was quite spontaneous and unexpected. Ryan described one instance: "I noticed that before starting my journal I was just sitting with the images, and I was sitting with Monk and the cobra, movement started happening." A similar thing happened when he did his written dialogues between the two images. "A lot of the dialogue was about how do we make this integration happen, because it seems like they feel separate, but they don't necessarily need to be and that maybe them finding harmony would be helpful. So it feels like in some really subtle way it is sort of happening, in that even if I feel differently looking at them, they're kind of like cross-pollinating a little bit. It feels like some sort of synthesis or emerging is happening."

Ryan noticed that he "definitely felt more energized and more clear and less cloudy." He also mentioned that Nathaji had directed him to work on bringing the kundalini from his heart space to the center of the head. The phenomenological experience of this shift felt very different for Ryan. His focus included the heart, but his heart was experienced spatially at the bottom of a larger heart space, while his head was experienced as the center of that larger heart space. Even looking out with open eyes from this new energetic space felt different to Ryan.

During the time between our interviews, Ryan wrote four active imagination dialogues in his journal.[iii] The first one he did with Monk,

---

[iii]Active imagination is a technique developed by Jung in which the contents of the unconscious are allowed to surface, and are rendered in image, dialogue, movement, or other creative expression, in order to integrate them into the psyche more consciously.

the second with Cobra, and the third and fourth were dialogues between Monk and Cobra. There was a sense of movement and integration with each dialogue, but the most palpable shift occurred in the third and fourth dialogues.

In Ryan's first dialogue with Monk, they seemed to encounter each other tentatively, shyly, with a little nervousness. Ryan asked Monk if there was any advice to impart to him, and Monk replied, "Leave the dark cave for the light. See that light and the noise and chaos of things which initially feel repellant. Let go, listening to the calls of the body." Ryan was surprised by that advice from Monk. Contemplating the dialogue later, there were some parallels with Monk advising him to let go, and some areas in which he still felt stuck in his life. Monk was a "a figure of those weighty, hurtful holding on [to things] that sort of have to be let go of finally."

He then read aloud the second dialogue with Cobra. Cobra usually came, even while doing the dialogue, with physical sensations—like the urge to move, or heat in Ryan's body. There was something very elemental and energetic about Cobra, arising with a sense of timelessness. For instance, when Ryan asked Cobra what happened when he first appeared in Ryan's experience in India, Cobra replied, "Cobra looked through you, some things long dormant woke up." Interestingly, in his dialogue with Monk, Ryan asked for advice, but in his dialogue with Cobra, Ryan asked how better to serve the image of the cobra, and asked what he could offer the image. When Ryan asked that question, Cobra replied, "Continue as you have been, open your heart. Work, hunt, move continuously as the serpent does in rhythm with pulse." In contemplating that response from Cobra, Ryan felt that he needed to continue to cultivate the energy that came with Cobra, perhaps through movement—whether in a physical way or in a subtler and more internal dimension. "Kind of like whatever the movement, just keep moving, maybe like continuing the movement and then building upon it, rather than getting it and then leaving it and then trying to come back to it. It's being more in tune with it and keeping it."

In the third dialogue, Monk and Cobra encountered each other directly. The first question asked each other what their image conveyed. Monk replied that he was "the call to look within, the struggle of that journey, but also the poise, the grace, the regality that God can possess, although beyond attribute." Cobra's sense of what his image conveyed was "energy that cannot be contained, that will not remain still, contained, or transfixed." They had a small talk about integration, and how to do it, almost as if Ryan was just a third party in the room and they were having a chat on his behalf. Monk and Cobra decide a ritual might work, an external action in service to the unity of these different energies becoming more apparent. Cobra suggested, "I could move into your cave, that way then we may cohabitate in this gross physical way and rub off on each other." By "gross" physical body, Cobra, who is light and movement, was referring to a heavier, denser manifestation of the body.

Ryan mentioned that he had spontaneously encountered many images of cobras during the last month. These cobra "sightings" did not necessarily occur when he was thinking about Cobra, but they occurred frequently enough to feel a bit uncanny. They seemed to indicate repeated events of synchronicity, which was Jung's term for meaningful coincidences when something experienced in the inner world then manifests in the outer world, usually with an archetypal dimension. The archetypal image of Cobra showing up again and again in Ryan's external world during this time when he was exploring Cobra's energy in his internal world was meaningful to Ryan.

On one occasion while driving, Ryan heard the lyrics "going to go like a cobra coil" from one of his favorite bands, Wilco, playing on the radio. Then a bit later Ryan was watching a documentary on India, and the narrator was talking about the author Rudyard Kipling. A cover of one of Kipling's books flashed on the screen—it was the author's name and a giant cobra. In another instance in a similar timeframe, Ryan's partner was going through a newsfeed with Ryan over breakfast, and there was a story of a journalist who saved about 600 cobras; for Ryan, it was yet another meaningful instance of the image of cobras making themselves present.

It didn't just occur in the first month—it happened during all three of the months we worked together. For example, a few days after our second interview, Ryan sent me a photo of a giant, colorful, ceramic cobra he had encountered while shopping at a plant nursery. During our third interview, Ryan mentioned again that a cobra popped on the screen of his TV, in an advertisement for an Indiana Jones movie coming to a cable network. The picture was of Harrison Ford as Indiana Jones, staring face-to-face with a cobra. And finally, one day after our interviews were complete, I encountered a cobra with Ryan. I was talking with Ryan and his partner after meditation class one evening when his partner showed me a book he was reading—a cobra was on the cover. I glanced up at Ryan and we shared a smile.

In the fourth dialogue, the conversation between Monk and Cobra deepened; it was by turns more intimate and yet more spiritually philosophical. They began by greeting each other as two beings picking up a thread from a previous, though unfinished, conversation. Both Monk and Cobra acknowledged that some merging or harmony had begun to occur, and that at its core, it "is all God after all." Cobra elaborated on this thought by saying, "It is all one thing, I am the movement of that thing." Monk responded to Cobra, "I am the phase before death and immortality, the symbol of the final look one takes at things earthly. In a way, you could call me a guardian or keeper of sorts, this essence one must master and move on."

Cobra asked if there is death for Monk, but Monk felt that death was just another transformation, while Cobra felt that there was no sense of death he could conceive of. They both inquired how to help Ryan further with this integration of energy, and Cobra said, "It is up to him . . . he must be with all manifestation thrown his way, as we are with each other: compassionate, humble, gentle in love, fierce with good intent." And as the dialogue wound to a close and they said their goodbyes to each other, Monk ended the conversation with, "Until we meet again, my friend."

I felt deeply curious about what Monk said regarding immortality and being a symbol for the last bit of earthly things, and asked Ryan to say more about it. He replied, "I just see that as the transition from limitation to eternity to representing that last step towards being a manifested being, before transitioning into an unmanifested being, like a symbol of those of us in separation wanting to get out of it. It's the desire for something to go back to its source or a symbol of the person dedicated to look within, a person dedicated to find truth, a person dedicated to discover themselves."

I asked Ryan if this meant one must be very internally focused to do this, like Monk. Ryan replied, "Yeah, or just having the ability to look within or the desire to look within and see, just staring through these patterns, or like karmic projections. Sort of stopping, just looking for something more. I think he's a symbol of that work." "Monk," he continued, "is like a more relatable bridge in a way. It kind of has aspects of both, the way that Cobra is like unbounded and Monk has this divine aspect, but also a human aspect."

I asked Ryan to enter into a drawing exploration that expressed this new inner sense of beginning the process of integration. This image resulted.

Awakening

The vividness and energy in this picture was notable, even palpable. The same colors of Monk—the blue, purple, black and open white areas are still present, but the colors of the original cobra drawing—red, yellow, green, and blue—seem to spurt forth in a powerful blast through the third eye chakra. Monk's eyes seem to be partially open and his face is much more clearly defined. Ryan and I both felt like Monk seemed less remote, more human and accessible.

I asked Ryan what he felt about the image. Initially, he noticed that the lines of the face were more precise and stronger. I mentioned that Monk looked more present, and I appreciated the vividness of all the colors, and it appeared that Cobra's colors were coming out of the

Monk's head. Ryan said, "Cobra's taking the quickest route, jumping right through him."

I mentioned that Monk's faced looked more peaceful. Ryan responded, "I'm also noticing his eyes are really far apart, which a lot of times babies and young people, their eyes seem really far apart and the get more narrow. So in a way he almost looks more youthful than the other picture that looks a little more aged in a way." I remarked that in the first picture of Monk, he looked ancient and mummified to me, but this Monk looked more human, more like a middle-aged man. I asked Ryan if he would name this image, and immediately he replied, "Awakening."

I suggested that since Monk and Cobra had discussed doing a ritual together to manifest their beginning integration on a concrete, external level, that Ryan conduct such a ritual during the month before our final interview. I also suggested that he continue with any dialogues or writing that he might feel compelled to do, and he agreed to the idea.

The Third Interview

Six weeks after the second interview, Ryan arrived at my office for our last interview with a ready smile and I felt pleased and happy to see him. Personally, I felt like a warm connection had developed between Ryan and me, and perhaps even between Monk and Cobra along with Ryan and me. I was eager to engage with all of them again.

In an overall sense, Ryan conveyed that during the time between our second interview and the final one, his writing was more general, less focused on one particular image of Monk or Cobra. "It feels looser in a way," he said, "compared to the last couple months. I noticed a sense of putting it together. It was a little less focused and a little more, 'this is how these things are popping up in all these different places.'" Ryan noticed it was harder to specify the distinct figures of Monk or Cobra, and harder to pull them apart as separate entities. He felt that this perhaps indicated a kind of blending of the energy between the two images.

We turned to Ryan's writing dialogues which were fewer in number then at our previous interview. However, he read aloud a particularly compelling writing interaction that he had with Monk. Ryan was sitting in a cafe without his drawings, so he conjured the image of Monk from his imagination. To his surprise, Monk appeared with an entirely different visual and energetic resonance. "It was really bright-eyed and really smiley and just this glowing thing. I didn't feel any less authentic than looking at the drawing and contacting it. It felt like the same thing, but it had this really different feel. It's this very romantic, happy, bright figure coming out. It's interesting. To me, that almost says that it has some of Cobra's aliveness or that Monk was getting what he wanted or something happened that was really favorable to this relationship."

Ryan recounted some of the actual dialogue he had with Monk at the cafe, and it is notable in its beauty. The images in this dialogue were of an outside landscape, whereas prior to this dialogue, Monk had been in a cave. In the dialogue, Ryan asked Monk to comment on this new glowing energy and happiness that emanated from him. Monk smiled and said he felt joy and bliss that would arise and subside, and that "the summer sun is bright, the winter moon most crisp." Ryan responded to Monk by commenting that his inner landscape at that time had felt very wintery. He asked Monk how to function during such times. Monk replied, "Get to know the cold. The shiver of the body from chill is a kind of beauty, of bliss. The snow covers the forest in elegant splendor, and the melt, you will appreciate the freshly revealed colors of the wilderness more fully . . . see the ice as transformative light. You are brooding, as final preparation to bloom." Ryan remembered feeling rather surprised by Monk's poetic turn. He couldn't think of what else to ask Monk, so he inquired whether there was anything Monk wanted to add that would break the "spell" of the dialogue. Monk said, "Why break what is thriving? Why destroy prematurely what is just come to life?"

I felt quite moved by this dialogue and the beautiful images of the landscape that Monk conveyed. I shared with Ryan that the images of the forest and nature were compelling to me. Ryan replied, "It's interesting to hear the servant in the cave talk so freely about the forest and wilderness. It almost seems like Cobra, animal." I commented that I felt a shift in Monk. Before, I imagined Monk held a quality of stillness that was sad and solemn, and now that quality of stillness felt more serene and clear, with a quiet beauty emanating from it. Ryan felt that the energetic quality of Monk had transformed to a more poetic feel, like the literary Romantics. Ryan recalled, "It just had this really deep wisdom, but also like a love for the world. I think I could find deep beauty and wisdom and truth in these really natural things. I like this side of Monk."

Ryan also showed me drawings he had done during the month. He had drawn them spontaneously, without a strong objective in mind. Often, Ryan would draw or doodle this way, letting the image or images appear spontaneously, without an initial concept in mind. He showed me the drawings he had done during a week where he had spent some time with his partner in a house in the mountains that offered relaxing time away from the city, surrounded by nature. It's a particularly compelling image that related to our work together.

New Depths

I found myself transfixed by this drawing. It appeared Monk and Cobra had integrated in a particularly enlivened way. Ryan and I were both struck by the serenity on Monk's face. It looked as if Monk's eyes were rolled back in a profoundly deep meditation, with a small smile of pleasing tranquility playing around his mouth. We were both delighted by the direct gaze of Cobra, peering out of the picture towards whoever might be looking. In Ryan's words, the cobra in the drawing was saying, "Yeah, I'm here." Cobra is also coming out of the center of the head, traditionally the bindu point, or seed and central point, of the head chakra. The graffiti script style title of the drawing is "New Depths."

One last synchronicity involving Cobra occurred during the time between our second and third interviews. Ryan had come across a book called *The Path of Fire and Might* by Swami Rama. As he flipped through the book he didn't relate to a lot of it, but there was one chapter on kundalini that he dove into reading. One of the first things in that chapter was a breakdown of the word "kundalini" in Sanskrit. Ryan explained, "The term kundalini comes from the Sanskrit word 'kundala,' which means coiled. It also related to the word 'kunda,' meaning a bowl used for sacrificial fires. And as soon as I read that, I thought of the first cobra drawing and it has that little green, round bowl. All of the other figures in the drawing are really blasting and non-linear and this was a really clear, round bowl shape."

When creating his ritual of integration that I had suggested he conduct before our third interview, Ryan traced the first drawing of Cobra and put it into a green bowl, or kunda. He also put a Shiva-Lingam statue he bought in Ganeshpuri, right after his kundalini experience, next to the bowl. Ryan lit incense and a candle and bowed to all the drawings, then bowed to the bowl with the cobra drawing in it. He then burned the drawing in the bowl. While performing this ritual, Ryan stayed aware of the physical sensations happening in his body. He noticed a "weighty energy" and a swaying movement that often accompanied Cobra. However, this time it was subtle, not just from the head. According to Ryan, "It was almost like the shoulder, core body kind of sway. So it was pretty subtle and pretty sweet and just a little basic, getting all my little things together . . . it just seemed like all these different elements that are overlapped."

Ryan noted that after the ritual, and as time progressed, the separateness of the cobra and monk image was dissolved. "What struck me, if anything, is just how it was really hard to pull back and focus on an individual part . . . it felt energized and it felt open, but it didn't necessarily feel like all these separate, interacting pieces. It just felt like this bigger, open feeling." I asked Ryan how this process of working together with these images had impacted his spiritual practice, if it had at all. He felt that it helped him deepen his connection with the practice and helped him relate to the term "kundalini" more, "like having a name or a feeling or a figure that I can connect to. Because oftentimes, when it gets into a discussion of Tantra terminology, I get really checked out and just have a really hard time feeling anything from it. So this has helped me see how that energy can work in a subtle way that isn't necessarily limited to this definition or have to be understood through this context of scholarly discourse." Ryan also felt that the process made him less suspicious and wary or hesitant of all the terminology and philosophy around kundalini because the mental or intellectual obstacle had transformed into a personally lived experience that he could relate to.

Our time together had come to a close. It felt difficult to end. I had come to know Ryan more deeply, but also to make the acquaintance of some very special and wise images that had become living entities for me, as I imagine they had for Ryan. As he stood to go, we both hesitated, feeling a little sad that the work was complete. It was a sweet moment, and as we hugged goodbye, I felt tremendous gratitude for being allowed to witness and explore with Ryan his process with kundalini and these images. Later, when I would see Ryan in meditation class, it was as if Monk and Cobra were present with him, not as visual images, but as psychic entities sharing space with him.

I imagined that this is true for all of us—that we have a collection of images and entities that populate our psyches and act as our friends and teachers in many ways. If they could appear in the room as they appear in our psyches, we might experience a rich and wide spectrum of aliveness that we normally don't perceive. I was grateful to get to peek behind the veil of the conscious mind and witness just a little bit of that. These are my impressions, but I think it is appropriate to end with Ryan's own thoughts on kundalini that he wrote in his journal prior to our second interview.

Ryan wrote, "Shakti-Kundalini, that unseen but directly knowable force permeates all things, could be said to be all things we encounter in manifestation. Some subtle vibration, some resonance, some unexplainable vitality alive, awake, awe inspiring, and joyful, completely intimate, yet elusive. Palpable, but seemingly uncontained. This body or planet or existence is some storehouse of spiritual material, God's tool shed. A love so unconditional, it defies static form. Perhaps that is part of the joy found within that energetic current, the freedom entire, that no rest or reprieve occurs, no chance to capture or conceal by analytical operations, this all-powerful thing. There is this all-pervasive, serene stillness, and then moving in, through, or of this stillness, some quality emerges. It is not dead or dull or non-stillness; it is not unsatisfying silence; it is miraculous through no other reason than that it is inherent nature, it's not just dead air. It's like there's something and my sense is that, the longer you do this work, the more you can feel it and the more intricate and deep and varied and the word intoxicating—but that might not be the right word—but just the more rich it becomes."

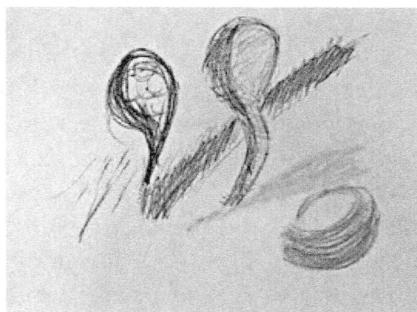

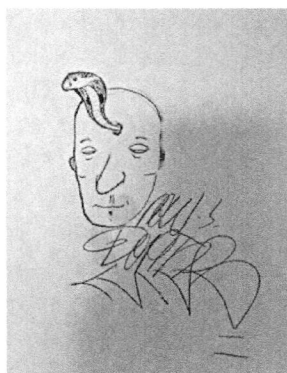

Reflections on Ryan's Story

From a Jungian and archetypal perspective, the overarching theme of psychological and spiritual work during this period of Ryan's life seemed to be integration. The image of the cobra is a common archetypal image in Indian mythology and a symbol for kundalini in Tantric philosophy in particular. In these images, one often sees the cobra rising up from the spine to the top of the head and hovering behind the head. The cobra for Ryan seemed to presage the immanent eruption of kundalini energy in him. The cobra image and consequent kundalini awakening was also

71

an initiatory energy that didn't squelch a psychological complex of mistrust, rather it intensified it, creating a tension in the oppositional psychic energies of movement and stillness, engagement and withdrawal, and trust and mistrust, which also expressed itself as an issue of belonging in the community. However, it is the additional image of the monk that allowed the tension of opposites to be felt and experienced, and therefore integrated.

We can see the polarity of the images both in the visual representation of Ryan's drawn images and the descriptions of those feelings. For instance, Monk is weighty and still in juxtaposition to Cobra's lightness and continuous movement. Monk sits low in Ryan's body, like a boulder, and appears dark or black in color, while Cobra is full of color and is situated in the heart and head areas. Monk, at least initially, prefers the quiet and the dark—he sits in his cave shunning light and chaos. Cobra is rhythmic, chooses to "work and hunt," and has a sense of spacious openness.

In the first interview, Ryan felt that the energy of the two images was completely separate, "like oil and water," and sensed that the energies could be integrated. Through his journaling and working with his body in between our interview sessions, Ryan began to notice a shift occurring. The separate energies were still distinct in quality, but there was a sense of the underlying energy consisting of the same material. When Ryan sat with the monk image at home, his body spontaneously began to sway back and forth, like the undulations of a cobra. A sense of openness as well as emptiness began to emerge. This new beginning sense of merging and integration culminated in an externalized ritual— as suggested by the images themselves in the active imagination dialogues. During our work together, Ryan used both movement and dialogue between the images as a form of active imagination. In doing so, the wishes of the unconscious emerged and blended with the conscious mind. The physical ritual created a concrete, external expression for the newly conscious integration that was unfolding.

By the third interview a larger shift had taken place. New imagery arose in his journal entries of seeds and nourishment. One journal entry evoked the inner image of a seed. Ryan wrote, "One feels spiritual energy or divine nourishment pour into the seed as light or water into the vegetal. Moving more deeply within a very clear sense of roots descending from the seed and filling the body . . . This root system feels particularly developed around the heart, but can be perceived throughout the entire body below the head. Through limbs, toes, extremities, organs. Nourishment pours into the seed and courses through the root system. . . . Above the head is felt as pure creative potential. As if within the seed the awaiting organism knows entirely the extent to which it can grow."

The imagery is both organic and vegetative. A seed is being deeply nourished by water. Water images are chiefly symbols of the unconscious, but coupled with images of light, the water image also points to the numinous nature of the experience of the transformation of psychic energy through the transcendent function. The water coursed through the whole root system. Of the image of water, Jung wrote,

> Water is the commonest symbol for the unconscious. The lake in the valley is the unconscious, which lies, as it were, underneath consciousness, so that it is often referred to as the 'subconscious,' usually with the pejorative connotation of an inferior consciousness. Water is the 'valley spirit,' the water dragon of Tao, whose nature resembles water—a yang in the yin, therefore, water means spirit that has become unconscious.[36]

In Ryan's exploration, I would argue that the numinous water flowing into the seed was the unconscious becoming conscious, and also a possible indication that the kundalini energy—often described as liquid light or golden, sweet nectar—was illuminating the whole mind-body system.

There is additional striking imagery in Ryan's later journal entries that speak to his sense of the integration of the images and the archetypal energy they express. He wrote, "Gazing upon the third and final drawing of this exploration, the word comes: integration. There is some subtle sense of all things resembling separation or distinction as a flimsy foundation upon which some curtain has been displayed. Lift the edge and peer beneath. Destroy the latch by which the fabric is held and let it fall. Beyond? A screen of pure openness. A clear convoy of unlimited potential."

There is a sense of revelation in this journal entry. For Ryan, the veil dropped to reveal a deeper understanding—the two energies held within the images, which had previously seemed separate, were of the same substance. The veil also seemed to harken back to the image of Monk, perhaps in heavily veiled clothing, being seen through and ultimately dropped, so that a sense of openness and potentiality was revealed.

In one of the final journal entries, Ryan did free writing on his experience of kundalini. Ryan described kundalini as "stillness that is pregnant, teeming and filled of some living force." There is a reference to death and rebirth in his continued description, as well as moving from the personal to an impersonal, more cosmic sense of the energy. Ryan wrote, "Moving into it [kundalini] one can just feel a certain drop, or depth of experience, and then—BOOM! Life, potentiality, creativity. Artful currents of numinous force awaiting regeneration and birth. Exploding into the periphery of the world like an extinguished star."

Ryan's interviews, drawings, and journals beautifully describe how the process of and work with kundalini mirrors the process and work that occurs in the alchemical stages of the psyche's transformation. It's as if kundalini is both the potent precursor of the archetypal images, as well as the impetus and driving force for the manifestation of the archetypal forces. As we may have many psychic death and rebirth experiences in a lifetime, so might we experience alchemical changes in the psyche more than once, as the psyche spirals ever deeper to reveal more complexes and more opportunities for integration, leading us toward the wholeness of individuation.

CHAPTER SIX

Colleen's Story:
Terror, Curiosity, Connection

I like to think that I met Colleen through a dream. Colleen and I both lived in Jakarta, Indonesia, in 2015, but even though we were on the same group email list for expatriates, we didn't know each other. One night I dreamed that I was crossing a bridge of light, and below me, watching me, was Nathaji, my spiritual teacher. He said to me, "You're full of love and you know who you are, now you just need to let that energy circulate through your whole self." I woke up feeling an enormous surge of love and peace. I decided that doing a Qi Gong or Tai Chi practice would be another way to let this energy circulate through me, and so I sent an email to the expatriate group list asking if anyone knew of any classes in my area. Colleen said she'd be interested in similar classes, and also wanted to know if anyone was teaching meditation. I wasn't teaching meditation at the time, although I was in training to become a meditation teacher for Nathaji. Since the request was made, I decided I would answer it and teach for anyone who wanted to attend.

The morning of the meditation class, I did my own solitary meditation practice. I centered myself in my heart, allowing myself to relax and open. What was immediately present was a sense of Nathaji. It was as if his energy was resonating inside me. I quieted my mind further and relaxed around the very palpable experience of my teacher residing in my heart. Like a body of water, the resonance between my teacher and I seemed to deepen and spread out simultaneously. I felt completely merged with his energy, and also connected to a larger, more cosmic energy field. I felt a sense of complete belonging—to myself, to Nathaji, and to the universe. Any sense of separateness, aloneness, or isolation dissolved totally. The rest of that morning and afternoon and during the meditation class I taught, I was suffused with the sweet, pulsating energy of shakti-kundalini. It gently washed through me, suffusing my body on a cellular level. When the meditation participants arrived, I was in a quietly blissful and peaceful state.

Three or four people came to my meditation class, one of whom was Colleen. Meeting Colleen was like having a ray of sunshine stream through my door. She is tall and elegant, with intelligent, lively blue eyes, and a quick, bright smile. Colleen thoughtfully and graciously had a gift of incense she offered me for teaching the class. I did a simple class that afternoon, guiding people through the chakra system, having them envision bringing light to each center and guiding them to relax and let go. I didn't have any expectation that anyone would experience kundalini, since that's something that usually happens over time. The most I hoped to achieve by guiding the class was that people had an opportunity in their busy lives to slow down and to tune into themselves. After class everyone thanked me, including Colleen, and went on with the rest of their day.

But for Colleen the meditation was more profound. She described it in our first interview: "What I want to say about the meditation was that my experience was profoundly relaxing and energizing at the same time, and I felt like everything was open. My heart, my mind, and everything around me was very open. It was really a beautiful place to be. It carried on throughout my day, in that I had a very beautiful experience and breakthrough with my eleven-year-old son that day. I had been very guarded and worried about him being kidnapped in Jakarta and I actually made a decision to let him go to tennis with our driver without me. It was a decision made from this spaciousness, from this feeling of connectedness. I was connected to everything and all is well. All is well. It was a beautiful experience for me and it was a beautiful experience for my son, and when he returned he seemed taller in his stance and I just felt like, 'Gosh, this is just beautiful. The experience from this morning is just continuing on.'"

Colleen felt that her son was "taller," meaning he had some pride in being allowed to attend tennis without his mother escorting him there for protection, and she felt very good about her decision for both of them. It was a weighty decision to make because during our residency in Jakarta, two school teachers and five Indonesians who had been hired for janitorial service had allegedly sexually abused a five-year-old boy in the International School's bathroom. The International School's community and the Indonesian community were all profoundly upset and frightened. Colleen's concern for her son's safety was impacted by those recent events.

Colleen continued, describing her experiences later in the evening and into late night. "My husband was out of town, it was just my son and me, and I put my son to bed. I thought, 'Okay, I need to get to bed too, but I am not tired.' I felt incredibly energized. It felt like I had so much caffeine to drink, but I didn't have the jitters. I felt like I could run a marathon, and it's 9:00, 9:30, 10:00. I thought, 'I need to go to bed, I have to get up super early.' Back downstairs, I'm cleaning up, trying to do things to make myself tired, but I was feeling 'Wow, I just have so much energy, what am I going to do with this?'"

She answered that question by walking back and forth in her living and dining room, sharing, "I was running, walking fast, just trying to get myself tired. Now, this is not normal. Nothing like that ever happened before. I've never had an experience like that before. Finally I said, 'Okay, I'm going upstairs and I'm going to force myself to go to sleep.' I was lying on my back and thoughts would come and go and I was agitated. It felt like I couldn't calm down. At this point, I don't remember if I fell asleep or not, but finally there was peace and my eyes were closed, and then I had this sense of an enormous amount of energy bursting. There was a tunnel of energy perpendicular to my body above the lower part of my legs up to the ceiling, down through the bed. I saw it and I was frightened, and then I was thinking to myself, 'What is going on, what is this?'"

She described looking around and thinking, "'Well, this is curious.' It was like hundreds of thousands, if not millions, of these little tubes, just energy—I don't know how to describe it—moving up and down, up and down, all around and it was like a force field. It was incredibly powerful and very foreign. It was almost, in some ways, alien-like, but I don't mean like an alien. I mean I'd never seen anything like this before, and this energy was encapsulated in a circular, tubular form, and I vacillated between being very intrigued and absolutely terrified. I would close my eyes and I'd open them and it was still there."

Colleen didn't have a sense of how long this lasted. "I really can't give you a timeline," she said. "I don't know. I would play with my eyes back and forth and close my eyes, open my eyes, and then finally I said, 'You've got to get some sleep.' And it was really interesting because as I said, 'All right,' one part of me was tired and I just knew that part of me was going to sleep, but the other half of me was completely awake. The eye on my 'awake' side was actually open and that half of my body was fully awake, but the other side of my body seemed like it was sleeping and the eye on that side was closed. I was very aware that part of me was awake and part of me was asleep."

I asked Colleen if she felt a sense of presence with the light, and she said she didn't, but that she was "cognizant of energy, this incredibly powerful energy." And though eventually she did fall asleep, right before she did so she reported "sensations of popping sounds and hearing sounds like ringing bells."

When Colleen finally fell asleep, she had a very vivid nightmare. Colleen recalled, "It felt like the most evil energy in the universe was after me, and it was smoke-like. I didn't smell smoke, but it was like smoke was enveloping me and the most evil elements of the universe were seeking me, and then Blondie's song started playing very loudly. The song 'I'm going to find you, I'm going to get you, I'm going to get you, get you, get you,' just loud, and I just remember feeling, 'Oh, my gosh. I'm not safe in this world.' And then I had an experience, because of inner child work I've done in the past, I had an experience with my inner child and my inner teenager . . . and they were incredibly angry and said to me, 'You told us we were safe in this universe.' Then the dream subsided, that was done, and I had sensations and I had more noises."

"What were the sensations?" I asked.

She answered, "A couple of jolts and some loud-pitched noises. That's what I remember now. Then, I think I slept after that and when I woke up in the morning I was absolutely—I didn't know what to think and I was quite disturbed actually, and I contemplated, 'Maybe this is an antibiotic reaction because I've never had anything like that happen before.' I did not think of it as a blissed out experience. However, I will say this: I thought, too, that it was a gift to have an experience like the pillar of energy like that, this incredible amount of energy, like not able to explain it from an everyday perspective and experience. I did feel left with, 'Wow, there is so much going on in the universe' that it left me in awe and in wonder and in great mystery, and I think that's a gift. I guess that's how I would describe the experience."

The First Interview

In the time between Colleen's experience and meditation and our first interview together, we had become good friends. Colleen left Jakarta at the end of 2015 and returned with her husband and son to Houston, Texas. By the time of our first interview, I had also returned with my husband, settling in our home in California. I flew out to Texas to interview Colleen in her home. We settled into her cozy family room, listening to the rain hit the windows in a summer downpour.

After she described that first experience of kundalini, I asked Colleen to take a moment and feel into her body, noticing any thoughts, emotions, or sensations that were present. She responded by saying, "What's present is a joy in my heart and a feeling of deep gratitude, because I feel like the experience was not only a gift, but has been an ongoing gift, and so I feel very warm and grateful." I asked her if she could speak to how the experience was an ongoing gift. She settled in and offered a detailed response.

"Well, there are lots of different things that happened because of that. I know that this is not psychotherapy, but some of the conversations I've had with you helped clarify that experience. For instance, when we discussed one possible interpretation of such a petrifying dream. It's like, well that's just some of the unfinished business that you still need to work on and I'm at a point in my healing and development where I am able to do so now. I felt like I've had some peace with maybe there's not such evil in the world. Based on past experiences, there've been a couple times I just tried to understand what I would interpret as evil and that I wasn't safe. I think my experience has been the process of uncovering and seeing that, 'Wow, some things have happened, but maybe not because of evil, but because some bad things happened, and I'm okay.' And that's a huge gift. So that's one example."

She continued, "Another is that I feel like my curiosity has been piqued greatly and I am in awe of this life and things going on all around and in me and other people and all living things seen and unseen. It's like this beautiful gift of deep curiosity. Really, instead of everyday life and humdrum, there is this profound mystery and so much that I don't know, and that's a gift. Another gift has been that sometimes I've felt incredibly alone in my life and I have a sense that I am not so alone in my life, and that I am connected."

Her voice became thoughtful as she shared the next part. "Another gift is that I have been able to share this with a very few, select people, because I feel like this has been a very precious experience, and that includes my husband and my son. It has led to some very deep conversations with them and a shared experience of awe and mystery. That's a double gift for me, because I don't always feel like we have an opportunity to provide that for our son, and it remains important to me to be able to discuss bigger questions about what is life about? What's it all about? How are we connected? What does it mean? Why are we here? It's led to some really interesting and beautiful conversations and it's opened the door, I think, for my son to consider the great divine and the loving energy in the universe, because he tends to be more scientific like his dad, and, 'Well, if you can't prove there's a god, then there's no god, Mom.' And so, he's more curious too now."

I asked Colleen how this experience affected her own personal, psychological work, which she had done a great deal of in the past. Colleen said that she had worked with several therapists and a life coach, but after the experience and discussing the nightmare with me, she found a somatic psychologist to work with, which was more intense than the past therapy or phone calls with her life coach in California. For Colleen, working with a somatic psychologist was "incredibly healing and helpful, and I feel like I'm in a whole different universe then I was two and a half years ago." Colleen knew that the work was an ongoing process, but she also felt like there was a "loving, healing energy that seems to be very present and is building and supportive and that all came from that experience with you in meditation and then that evening and afterwards."

I asked Colleen if she had any more experiences of energy since that first evening after meditation class. Colleen said that she hadn't experienced anything on that scale, but she did have some different experiences of sensations like vibration running through her body. She'd noticed the vibrating energy every two weeks or so. Colleen felt during those times that it was a reminder of how she was connected to the universe, reminding her that she was not alone. She then recalled a dream she'd had a few weeks prior to our interview that seemed to exemplify this newfound sense of connectedness.

She shared, "The dream involved my dad. It was an absolutely terrifying dream. I was hiding and I was with my husband and son, and my son didn't really know what the issue was, but they were trying to protect me. It's like, 'We're going to go out and look for your dad.' They went outside of the house to look for him and I thought to myself, 'He's here, he's here.' I opened the closet door and he was there. He was this incredibly frightening, not evil, just incredibly frightening energy. As I opened the door I was scared, and then the fear was gone, and I said calmly, 'You're here.' I said, 'Okay.' And then I walked away and I woke up from the dream and I was like, 'I'm okay. I am okay. He can't hurt me anymore. I might be afraid a little bit, but I can confront and be present and not shut down and I'm okay.' So it was actually very empowering, even though it was frightening, initially. I feel it was similar in my mind and heart to the experience of the terror I felt in the dream about the smoke looking for me as I was trying to get away. It was great because this time I was able to confront it. I had to do it on my own, too. My people went out and I had to do it myself, and I did do it. It was interesting. It's brought me a lot of peace."

I asked her to be present with her experience and feel into her body and see what was there, and Colleen said she felt peaceful. I asked if she would be open to doing some drawings. I suggested she draw the column of light, and perhaps the dark cloud from the dream, and Colleen agreed to do the drawings. I put on some music in the background, gave her art materials, and allowed about twenty minutes for Colleen to do her drawings. These were the drawings resulting from the process.

Smoky Disturbance

The Flow   *It's All Connected*

Colleen told me the first picture, which she later named "Smokey Presence," was acknowledging the sensation of the smoke in the first dream she reported having after the meditation class. The second image depicted the movement of the image of light that she saw while attempting to sleep that night. Colleen wanted the image to express the "form of movement, of just energy, but definitely an upward, downward, from my experience, and it was just flowing, just flowing." Appropriately, Colleen named that image "The Flow." Then the last image is of her impression when she was lying in bed. She folded the image in half, so there was a sense of her own body being horizontal while the tubular light was vertical at her lower legs. She said her body and the image were also connected to everything around it. She named the image "It's All Connected."

I then asked Colleen to move each image, going from one to the other when she felt like it. She started with the image "It's All Connected," and laid on her back on the floor, with her legs up and perpendicular to her body, similar to how the tube of light would have been when she was lying in bed. She flung her arms out to either side of her body, and she said it was holding circular space. Colleen noted during the movement process that she "really felt this tingling flow." She experienced herself as being in the middle of the flow, and that the energy continued on the other side of the floor in a connected and beautiful orb or circle. In a soft voice, Colleen said it was "like the whole universe is right here."

Next Colleen moved "The Flow" drawing. She moved in a happy wriggle on the floor with a great deal of energy, saying "I'm alive. Everything's coursing through me and I'm coursing through it. I can feel my heart beating and my blood is pumping. I know I'm alive, I'm aware of it, and I feel bliss." Colleen also felt like the sensation was of love, the very essence of all life that is everywhere and immediately present.

"I'll have what you're having," I joked. Then Colleen seemed ready to move on to the last picture, "Smokey Disturbance." She folded the page, saying that she felt that this image was just one page in a book that she was reading. Listening to Colleen, I felt that what once was a very scary image deflated in the presence of the love and the flow that was available with the other two images.

When I asked Colleen to move between two images, it seemed a little more challenging for her. As I described in more detail what I was thinking, Colleen curled on her side, like in a sleep position, but her feet flipped back and forth in a rhythmic motion. Spontaneously she put the image "Smokey Disturbance" underneath the image of "The Flow" and then put both images on her stomach. Then she added "It's All Connected" to the layers of the other two images, so that they were all together and lying on top of her torso. She began to rock forward and back against the length of her spine on the floor with a big smile on her face, then she flipped forward into a somersault. I asked her how that movement, which struck me as a jubilant, youthful movement, felt for her. "Well, I feel like a child of God, like I'm loved and cared for, and a part of and belonging to the love in this universe."

I asked Colleen if she felt complete, and when she indicated she was done with the movements, I asked her how the entire process of the interview, the drawing, and the movement was for her. She replied, "I think it's a really interesting process, and I'm grateful for this, to see how two years ago I was absolutely petrified, and the gifts that came from that experience and through our conversations and somatic experiencing therapy. All of that was just a page in a book. That's part of me, that's a part of the universe. It is not overwhelming but what's very present is this incredible amount of energy and connection and love."

The Second Interview

Colleen had been keeping a journal during the times between our interviews and she noticed she had written about more synchronicities. A notable one started with the name "Einstein" which appeared for Colleen an uncanny amount of times over the six weeks since our first interview.

I was present when "Einstein" initially showed up. We were playing a game with Colleen's family and some of her friends who had joined us for dinner on the last night before I left after her first interview. It's a simple game of putting a word on a piece of paper and sticking it onto someone's forehead, and each person takes a turn trying to guess the word put on them. I had put the word "Einstein" on Colleen's friend's head, because she was a scientist. We had a lot of fun playing the game. During the month afterwards, Colleen noticed that the name "Einstein" kept coming up.

The first Einstein quote she came across was in a weekly email of uplifting quotes she regularly received. The quote was, "Never lose a holy curiosity." A second synchronicity occurred while she was visiting a hobby shop with her son. A dog was visiting with its owner; its name was Einstein. The same day, Colleen opened an email with a quote from Einstein that read, "Energy is all there is. That means everything is guided by a source most people can't see, one that isn't easily measured or qualified." A few days later on a trip to the mountains, a woman hiked by Colleen with a coffee cup inscribed with "Einstein" on it. Another day, she read an article about finding one's passion in life. In the article there was a quote from Einstein, in which he says of himself, "I haven't special talent, I am only passionately curious." These synchronicities came in a very quick succession over a few weeks, making it feel more purposeful rather than a coincidence. Colleen felt that these synchronicities were a gift, pointing not to something given to her, but to gifts that she inherently possessed.

Returning to her journal topics, Colleen noted that she wrote often about her difficulty with drinking. Colleen drinks wine nightly, two or three glasses, and would prefer to drink less. When Colleen prepped dinner, she would have wine to relax. She realized she was very stressed out during that time of day in particular, and she connected that stress to the memory of her father coming into the kitchen and sexually assaulting her. She had been doing work with her therapist on reclaiming that space, so that the memory didn't come from behind and assault her, as her father had. This was new work for Colleen, and she felt she didn't have all the answers, but once again she remained open and curious to the process.

Colleen also said that she had used love, compassion, and forgiveness towards her father and the incest as a spiritual practice on different levels. Then, in what struck me as a powerful turn-around in the tone of the conversation, Colleen said that this love, compassion, and forgiveness "is not working for me. And that is one of the reasons I'm drinking. I am incredibly angry and that is in conflict with my spiritual aspirations to forgive and move on." I noticed a deepening in Colleen's voice as she spoke these words. Not a quality of anger, but rather of power. Her voice seemed to come from a deeper, fuller place in her diaphragm, and it struck me as having a great deal of authenticity to it.

Colleen continued, "The amount of anger that I have for my dad is so immense that I don't want to be present with it. It is terrifying to think that I have that much anger. And so it's like being down at your small pond and I walk around the edge of it—I walk around the edge of this anger. I don't dare step in because it would envelope me and I would be lost. I have a lot of sadness about that because part of me is like gosh, you've been in therapy for decades! Some people go shopping to keep the economy going. I just keep going to therapy."

Although it was a humorous comment about supporting the economy through therapy, Colleen was frustrated that she wasn't over the trauma, and she was frustrated that it affected intimacy with her husband. She became angry with herself for her avoidance strategies. Drinking was a way to keep the rage at bay, a way to not think about intimacy problems that were always linked to her father. Colleen then related a dream she had about a week before our second interview that seemed closely related to incest and anger, but also to her determination to keep going, to keep working.

She began, "I was at a meditation retreat with the Buddhist teacher Diane Hamilton. In attendance was a group of young 20s-ish boys who were very good looking and sexy. There was a lot of down time and I was able to walk about and even go on field trips. On one field trip, a bunch of us were riding a school bus or maybe it was just a bus. My neighbors across the street who are known to everyone in our neighborhood as really unfriendly because they don't participate in neighborhood street parties or events, were on the bus with me. A man started picking on his female partner. Initially, it was verbal abuse and then he began shoving her as they sat on the bus. Everyone just watched and no one got involved."

She continued, "Finally, I couldn't take it anymore. I got up and I grabbed the man out of his seat and told him to lay off the woman. Later, I returned to the retreat. I had to cross over a dangerous ravine by walking on a tree trunk and branches. It wasn't sturdy and there were large gaps, and many types of bugs crawling all over the place. There were a few other guys who would try to cross but they couldn't. And finally, I sat on my bum and I scooted across this ravine very slowly and I made it over and as I did a cloud of black flying insects tried to envelope me but it didn't stop me. At some point I found myself in a large and not very clean bathroom and I thought, 'Diane shower's here? It's dirty. I wonder who cleans this?' And as I walked about, I realized it was a unisex bathroom and someone was in a stall. It was a man and I ran away. I woke up and felt a pain in my heart and I told myself I would not have a heart attack because of this unfinished business with my dad."

Colleen managed to get herself back to sleep and found herself back in the dream at the retreat grounds where the first dream began. "My mom and dad who've actually been divorced for 30 years were there as a couple and they were happy. And I thought to myself, how come they're happy and I'm not? I'm still not happy and they are. And then I awoke and my first thought was I drink because I don't want to think about or feel how angry I am with my dad. I want to forgive my dad. It's my highest spiritual calling, I think. If I can create peace with my dad, there's hope for this world and all its craziness. But alas, I hate him. I don't forgive him. I'm angry enough that at times I could kill him. At night, cooking in the kitchen, which is when he would sometimes creep up on me, I start to drink and try to drown him and it out. And I'm drowning myself instead. Instead of killing him, I'm killing myself, slowly."

As Colleen finished reading her dream and her thoughts about it as she woke up, I found myself transfixed. It was a powerful dream and an even more powerful declaration of her deep feelings, and I managed to say, "Wow."

Colleen said, "So when you said we'd talk about the kundalini experience and this and that, I don't really know anything about kundalini. I've chosen not to read anything about it and just wanted to be present for my own personal experience. And what I'm seeing is I've obviously been just skirting issues that are there and I'm not moving forward in some ways and I just need to be with it, I need to work through it. I don't know how to do that. I'm working with a great therapist and I will. I will do it. I'm not going to stop my work. I think a part of that desire is from feeling connected and that this life is such a miracle—it's such a gift. Somehow, I am lucky enough to be able to witness it at times and not be stuck in the chaos. And also at the present, sometimes I'm very much in the chaos because it is—these are things that have happened to this particular incarnation in this life and there are lessons and things to learn and grow from. And I am so curious about that. And I feel some peace. And I even feel some peace around drinking and alcohol and obviously how I'm using that to skirt around the edges before I put my toe in and dive in."

I recalled to Colleen that she was both terrified and curious about her kundalini experience, similar to how she is terrified of her own anger on one level and also curious about it and the process of working with her trauma. I reminded her that she had sent me a beautiful picture from a friend that seemed to match her visual experience with kundalini, and I asked her if she could speak to either this sense of the terror and curiosity present in both situations, or the image she sent me.

She replied, "Well, what comes up immediately is that if I think back to March 2015 and the experience, what I find very interesting is that part of my dream experience that night was this gray smoke, evil energy, seeking me out, that I was not safe in the universe and it was going to get me and I was absolutely, positively petrified of that. Somehow, I equated that to my dad and evil. And how I feel about it now is, that's actually an incredible amount of anger that I have. I'm just projecting that onto my dad and things in the universe as if it is seeking me out. And I think I have this smoke of omnipresent anger and it can go anywhere, can just show up, out of control anger. And that's something that's really shifted for me. It's not out there; it's here, within me. And that's huge for me to see that. And back to your question, just now about the stream of energy. A woman I know passed away the week before last and her husband sent out a picture of this beautiful goddess within a stream of energy. My personal experience in Jakarta was like that. When I saw the picture I wanted to send it to you right away because I was like, 'this is it D, this is what I saw.'"

Colleen had sent me a picture of a goddess in a blue robe with a hood. The goddess was seated with her arms out at her sides with a column of light with thousands of small pearls of light descending from the sky, down through her head, and pooling in a swirling circle on her lap.

Colleen said the whole process of the psychological and spiritual work was subtle, and that she felt subtle internal shifts happening. In that moment sitting together, in a hushed voice Colleen said she wanted to be quiet and just listen. I suggested we take a moment to be quiet and to just notice what arose in the field of the body. Colleen closed her eyes, and almost as quickly her eyes popped open again. She exclaimed, "This is really—wow, I swear to you, this is crazy. When I closed my eyes, Rudi was sitting right where you are!"

Rudi—Swami Rudrananda—was my spiritual teacher's guru. There was a picture of him in the room behind where Colleen was sitting.

"That's wonderful," I said, finding myself sitting up a little straighter in my chair. "Can you—will you feel into that again? No pushing, just see what's present for you. I'm curious."

"Okay, so right now with my eyes closed—okay, it's gone now, but it was back. I could see Rudi, but just the shape of Rudi in orange and it was you as well . . . There was no sense of male or female. It was this energy, but it was very clearly Rudi and it was very clearly you."

"Wow."

"That's pretty cool," Colleen said.

"Yeah. Okay, thank you Rudi." I sent out a little mental thank you to whomever or whatever was present. This was certainly a surprise moment for both of us, but also very sweet. I never personally met Rudi; he died in a plane crash in 1972. But my teacher, Nathaji, was deeply devoted to him. From what Nathaji has said, and what I have seen in a few short films about Rudi, he was a powerhouse of shakti-kundalini energy. He was a fierce spiritual teacher, demanding much work from his students, but giving a tremendous amount of himself and love to his students in return. Rudi was a spiritual warrior. Somehow that seemed fitting for Colleen to see him, since she had done a lot difficult psychological and spiritual work that took a great deal of courage and strength to get to where she was.

Colleen said, "I don't normally have these kinds of experiences. I must tell you, that is pretty interesting! I also feel like what's present right now is that I'm in this flow. Instead of it being vertical, it's horizontal, and Rudi is here. His picture is behind me and you're here. And there's this—I'm caressed in this embrace of love and support, like just this beautiful universal—I'm in the hands of God. That's what's present right now."

Colleen also said she was clear that the work we were doing had a timeless quality to it, and also that she was no longer afraid of death. She had been afraid of dying in the past but that "this life, this work, this conversation, this experience, it already was, and it is, and it will continue."

The Third Interview

The third interview with Colleen was done over the internet two months after our second interview. I asked Colleen to describe anything that had come up regarding our work together in the last months. Colleen told me she had made a major decision to stop communication with her father and her father's second wife. It was a freeing experience for her, but it also took a lot of emotional energy to create the boundary. Colleen didn't feel like she knew how long this boundary would be in place, but she felt it was "key to me actually experiencing myself as in the flow, and flow is moving in and through me and that I'm not all stopped up."

I noticed that Colleen's body moved from a tightly hunched position and hands in fists when she spoke about being stopped up, to a more open and supple body movement when she talked about being in the flow. It was also interesting to me that she used the word "flow" because the experience of kundalini is often described in the same manner, as an energetic flow. I asked if there was a sense of opening that was associated with being in her own flow.

She replied, "Yeah. Being open, more creative, and more in touch with my energy that's flowing to the positive energy in the universe. I feel like a lot of that has been tamped down and I just won't let things in or out and keep things at bay, trying to squash thing and control things. It's just not working. I can see lots of old systems collapsing and breaking down. It's not working, which is great, because the point is by putting some healthy boundaries with some relationships in my life, I think that I can release some energy and be free."

Colleen described how difficult it had been to be in the presence of her father and his wife, because somehow the subject of incest was often obliquely brought up. It would be a conversation from the news, or a movie they had watched. It seemed as if it was unconscious energy in her father and stepmother's space that then leaked out when Colleen was present but would not be made conscious, and this was incredibly difficult for Colleen.

She described the difficulty. "I always feel like I have a muzzle on or someone's wired my jaw shut, and I can't be present for myself to represent myself, and then there's the angle of my spiritual self, that wants to "cause no harm in the world." If I speak out about it at this point, do I cause more harm? And so, that has been the dilemma for me, because I don't wish to cause harm, but then, what I'm seeing in therapy is that actually, I'm causing myself a lot of harm by not speaking, and it is costing me, when I squelch everything. I am disconnecting myself from that flow."

I asked Colleen how she might feel the kundalini was present in her life—was it like a flow or current moving through her life like a spiritual force and manifesting different ways, or did it feel like a separate incident that happened almost three years ago? She replied, "It was and is an ongoing incredible gift. And being a visual person, I'm so grateful that I had the experience of this color of light and energy and flow moving, because I bring that with me daily. When I talk with you, it's like 'Well, I have made some progress in this area or that area, and then I'm like, well, you know what though? It's been pretty amazing. It's been an amazing ride.' I'm really excited. Even though I go through these bouts of anxiety and depression and sadness and anger, it's like this circle and then it's like absolute gratefulness and joy and just a sense of freedom and flow. I guess when I'm present here, that's part of our flow too."

Colleen expressed gratitude to have worked with me—she felt we were "kindred spirits on the path." I mirrored back to her that grateful sentiment. While we ended the interview there, it felt like the work would continue on for both of us. The interview felt as if was a summation of the two previous interviews, but also hinted at future possibilities with her spiritual life as well as her personal and family life. The interviews were concluded, but the work would continuously move forward into her life.

Reflections on Colleen's Story

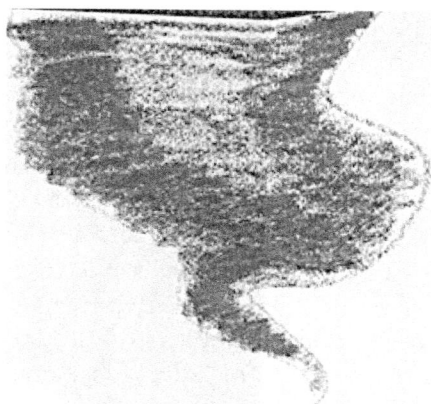

There are two very unique aspects to the work with Colleen and her kundalini experiences: first, kundalini might be experienced as a potential threat to and by a psyche that's experienced early trauma, as evidenced particularly by Colleen's first dream on the same night of the kundalini experience, and second, how *shaktipat*—the transmission of spiritual energy—can play a role in instigating a kundalini experience. In addition to these two aspects, Colleen's story shows the psychological impact that even one kundalini experience may have on a person over an extended period of time. For Colleen, kundalini ignited a deep curiosity and sense of connection to a larger reality, and consequently inspired her to work on her issues with more intensity and determination than ever before.

The work of Jungian analyst Donald Kalsched is particularly relevant and helpful when considering Colleen's experiences, particularly Kalsched's theory that the psyche's self-care system is similar to the body's immune system. In his book *The Inner World of Trauma*, he argued that when the regulation of trauma is not possible, the self-care system may attack itself, much like the body does with autoimmune diseases. In his experience working with clients, Kalsched observed a strong correlation between early trauma and a connection to a mythopoeic (myth-making), spiritual world. He noted that many such people have a strong kinship to nature, animals, and art of all kinds, but particularly poetry, and how these people "often report 'synchronous' experiences that defy rational understanding," and have "uncanny access to an immaterial reality that is inaccessible to better adapted people." These realms and experiences and presences are experienced as positive agents for protecting the psyche in trauma, Kalsched wrote. However, he also noted that over the lifetime of the trauma survivor, "the benevolent spiritual presences that seem to have saved their souls begin to lose their protective power. Under the pressure of repeated disappointments and disillusionments, these inner objects often turn malevolent. Inner protectors turn into persecutors."[37]

In the dream following Colleen's wakeful night of revved up powerful energy, with her vision of a column of effervescent light, she had a nightmare that evil smoke-like energy was after her. Then, her inner child and inner teenager, who were initially strongly positive images for her, reproach her angrily for not taking care of them. Colleen experienced them as frightening and also as tyrants of guilt because she didn't protect these inner vulnerable images. Kalsched wrote that in cases of early trauma, one part of the psyche may regress while another part progresses, and often the progressed part may show up in dreams by a powerful being who could be either benevolent or malevolent. One common symbolic image of this part of the psyche in malevolent form is a menacing cloud. During our interview process, Colleen did not mention spiritual experiences in childhood, yet I felt that her innate sensitivity and ease in accessing spiritual energy and a sense of being connected to a larger spiritual reality was a result of recruiting these larger energy fields or psychological realms because of early trauma with her father. At the same time, experiencing kundalini, however benevolent the energy is overall, was seen as a threat to the defensive part of Colleen's psyche.

In his book, *Trauma and the Soul*, Kalsched used the image of an Inuit storyteller's carved stone face to exemplify the "binocular" perspective needed to understand the two worlds of trauma survivors. The Inuit storyteller has one eye open looking outward towards the material, practical world, while the other eye is closed, focusing on the inner mythic world of images and imagination. This metaphoric image is paralleled in Colleen's experience with kundalini, when one of her eyes was closed and sleeping while the other eye continued to watch the energy before her. Perhaps one could say that the formation of this kundalini experience somehow mirrored a perspective and aptitude Colleen developed due to trauma. As Kalsched suggested, Colleen had the ability to connect to a very deep level of her psyche, perhaps initially as an adaptation to trauma when she was young, but now a connection that she could access with a certain amount of ease during meditation and dreams.

When speaking of her kundalini experience, and because of the dream that followed it, Colleen quickly shifted to talking about her traumatic relationship with her father, as if the spiritual experience and the trauma were intertwined. It was Colleen's innate curiosity that allowed her to have objectivity about the experience even as she was partially terrified of it. Her whole process over time working with the experience itself, and then letting it flow into deep psychological work with a somatic psychologist, and also sharing it with her family, reflects an iterative process of bringing the gems of learning from the spiritual or dream world to the practical reality of personal and family life, so that the outward reality could also develop and grow.

Over the time of our interviews together, we can observe through Colleen's dreams how she began to confront the malevolent energy. First, she saw it as a "stormy disturbance." She related a dream in our second interview where she alone confronts her father who is waiting for her in a closet. No one is there to help her, and even though she is afraid, she is able to confront her fear by herself. When working with the images of the dream and also with her kundalini experience in movement and drawing, the experience of "the flow" of the energy gave her a sense of connection to a larger whole—a sense of cosmic connection—which in turn helped her to look objectively at the disturbance without it overwhelming her. In a sense, the disturbance shrank in size as Colleen's sense of herself became connected to a larger sense of universality.

In the space between our first and second interviews, Colleen seemed to get in touch with a psychological strength that she possesses, which is curiosity. It is striking that Colleen had a series of synchronistic events in which she encountered quotes from Einstein related to the importance of curiosity. Synchronicities have a mysterious quality about them—it can seem like the universe is listening to the internal musings of an individual mind, and then responds in kind. These synchronicities seemed to cause a shift which allowed her to approach her continued work around the trauma and around spiritual experiences with a deepened sense of curiosity and wonder, which nullified at least some of the fear and anxiety around the work.

By the time of the second interview, Colleen had acknowledged her rage at her father. This was significant, as she had kept her rage suppressed because it seemed in opposition to her need to be a spiritual person that "did no harm." Yet Colleen realized that she was actually harming herself because she had directed the rage inward. She realized that the "smoky disturbance" of the first dream was most likely her own rage, or one might say using Kalsched's terminology that she realized that the image was the malevolent side of her psyche's wounded self-care system. In the dream she related during this interview, the character of Diane Hamilton, who is an idealized spiritual figure whom Colleen admired, became sullied in Colleen's mind because of the dirty bathroom. I interpreted this as Colleen moving away from an overly idealized, pure conceptualization of being a spiritual person. In the dream Colleen scoots on her bum across a dangerous ravine, while insects try and attack her. Here Colleen seems to be choosing a more humble, less idealized way to approach dangerous aspects hidden in the psyche, and though the insects—much like the smoky disturbance—try to attack her, she makes it across the ravine safely. At the end of the dream there is still some fear of a man in a dirty toilet stall, so we may assume the work with the trauma has not yet resolved, yet the psychological approach seems to have shifted from trying to remain pure and perhaps removed from the dirty realities of psychological and spiritual work, to getting down on the ground and humbly working her way through it.

As we talked, it seemed that Colleen's experience with kundalini, and her conjuring of that experience in memory, catalyzed her determination to keep working on her wounds, to resolve and free her own psyche and sense of connection to a larger universe, and also, I had a sense, for her family. For Jung, the connection to a larger sense of meaning was essential for psychological development, and for a sense of purpose. In *Modern Man in Search of a Soul*, Jung explored how the general cultural deterioration of belief in traditional religious systems necessitated the search for soul, or the inner exploration of psyche as a way to connect to larger meaning. Colleen's personal work and her experiences with a sense of the numinous underscore the importance of such work for a sense of purpose, and also as a wellspring of inspiration to continue exploring the psyche.

CHAPTER SEVEN

Jeremy's Story:
Fixing the Foundation

Not every encounter with kundalini begins with a spiritual intention or practice. Sometimes kundalini arises when the ego faces disintegration or collapses from a traumatic experience. These types of encounters can be difficult because without understanding what is occurring, they can compound the trauma by adding an uncontrollable, phenomenological experience that may feel like an invasion of one's individual identity. Fears of physical problems or insanity may arise. Such was the case for Jeremy, a gentle, soft-spoken man in his 60s, who encountered kundalini at a particularly low time in his life.

I met Jeremy around 2012, when he came to Swami Khecaranatha's meditation practice. Over the course of several years I noticed that Jeremy's experiences with kundalini in class seemed to have intensified, and I was curious about how the progression of his experiences both on a spiritual and psychological dimension, so I asked him to participate in my research study.

In his early 20s Jeremy trained as a yoga teacher, where he felt he had some brief experiences with kundalini energy. At the time of his major encounter with kundalini in 2008, Jeremy was feeling heavily impacted by the financial recession. The stress of the financial crisis started a downward psychological spiral for Jeremy that lasted several years—these traumatic events culminated in a kundalini experience.

The First Interview

Jeremy began his story with the recession in 2008 that greatly affected him. Things were difficult during that time, and to make matters worse, in 2009 Jeremy was diagnosed as HIV positive. His primary relationship with his partner was not going well. To alleviate the intense pressure of his stress and depression, Jeremy went to see a "sexual master." I didn't have knowledge of such a relational dynamic, so Jeremy explained it briefly to me. "This Master has slaves, other people that work there that work with him, live with him. He wanted to make me one of those. And so, at this one point when I was laying there I realized if I did what he wanted, I would have to give up my entire life and that seemed really dark.

Jeremy knew he didn't want to go that route, but he reflected that he must have "physically surrendered to the point where I had started having these bursts of energy coming up the base of my spine." While these spurts of kundalini were transpiring intermittently, someone in the group drugged him without his consent. The drug experience lasted for several days, in which Jeremy reported, "I was not able to sleep and I was speedy, and combined with that I was having these kundalini episodes."

Eventually the episodes which Jeremy described as "rushes" calmed down to a tolerable level, but continued to happen, which remained disconcerting for him. A friend of his who happened to be in the kundalini meditation practice pointed out that the symptoms he described sounded like kundalini, and suggested he come to a meditation class. Jeremy did not hesitate to go, in part because he was worried that "something neurological had been messed with because of the drug thing." He also just felt there was a "bottoming out to the whole thing. It was just like, okay, there's no more deeper down I was going to go than where I was." For Jeremy, this "bottoming out" also had an element of hope to it, because there was nowhere to go but up. Jeremy said, "Mixed with fear, there's also this hope of something." In his first experience sitting with Swami Khecaranatha, Jeremy noticed that the kundalini energy became more tolerable.

As Jeremy talked about the relief he felt coming to meditation class and his first weekend retreat, he had an intuitive flash about why he chose to see the sexual master. "It seemed like what would open me spiritually, and would open my heart was when I would have some love attraction to somebody. It would be my access to my spiritual place. I needed the love interests to have my connection to that part of me, so it was very frustrating. I think when I went to that master, I was just at an all-time low of really trying in some screwed up way to get into that part of me.

When I first started coming to the meditation class, and connecting with Nathaji, it was the first bit of getting 'oh, I can have this. I don't need another person for this.' Which is probably the biggest relief of all in this practice."

I asked Jeremy to stay with the feeling or memory of those kundalini rushes and see where they resided in the body. Jeremy said he felt the kundalini initiated in the first chakra. He began to rock back and forth in very small movements. He described the energy as moving in a counter-clockwise circle. As an emotion would come up, the energy would intensify. I asked him what emotion was present and he replied that it was sadness. He stayed with the sadness and the emotion itself began to feel like an unraveling. Then Jeremy described the energy as a kind of pendulum, but "the weird part is that the pendulum is upside down. My head is like the pendulum." I made sure I understood that Jeremy was saying the round part of the pendulum was in his head and the stem went down to his first chakra. Jeremy agreed with this description, and then, switching from the embodied and energetic observation, he wanted to talk about a series of dreams that were coming up for him.

Jeremy started with, "I'm thinking about my dreams lately with a twink theme."

"The Twix theme?" I asked, confused.

"The twink. Twink. That's what they call young, gay men—twink."

"Okay, twink."

"It's new terminology for you."

"That's right," I replied.

"These twinks are in my dreams, but they're not very important. They're in the background. There's this sexual energy always around, but there's other things that are focused on in the dreams, like houses."

I asked Jeremy to talk about a specific dream with a house in it. He described a dream from the prior week in which there was a house that was supposed to be renovated. The front of the house seemed fine, but when they went to the back, the whole side of the house was missing its foundation. Jeremy reported a feeling of surprise in the dream at the lack of foundation. In the dream he said to himself, "Wow, you've got to do something about that. How is this all being held up here?"

I brought Jeremy back to the body, asking him where he felt that lack of foundation. Jeremy replied, "It feels like the back side of my body doesn't have a foundation." Jeremy began to rock back and forth more vigorously in his chair. Then he said, "It's an earthquake." I confirmed with Jeremy that he just said it was an earthquake. "Yeah," Jeremy replied. "It doesn't seem to affect the house. Maybe the lack of foundation is good, otherwise it would break." Then Jeremy went still in his body and wondered if he should switch positions, but instead he remained still, noticing the presence of a lot of kundalini energy.

I asked Jeremy if he would be willing to draw his dream images and he agreed. This was the first image he created.

Master/House/Twink

While Jeremy was creating his images, I gave him some space and I went into the second room in my office and plopped down on the futon couch on my back, my arms out wide. I felt exhausted. I took a few deep breaths, and then got up to go back to the room. When I passed through the threshold of the doorway to the main office where Jeremy was drawing, it felt like the room was pressurized, like walking into a force field. I wondered if it was Jeremy, shakti-kundalini, or if it was the energy of the psyche that felt like a flexible bubble I was pushing against to get into the room. As Jeremy was finishing up his drawing I felt compelled to lie on the floor out of Jeremy's visual sight. It was then that I realized how much I was empathizing with Jeremy's wish to rebuild the foundation in his dream. It felt like a healing movement for me to be flat out on the solid foundation of the floor.

After completing the drawing, Jeremy described the different elements in the image. "This is the house with the back of the house where there's no foundation. You can see the foundation on the side." Then he pointed to the figure sitting on top of the house. "That's me on the house." And he pointed to the small smiling character in purple and then to the dark, frowning character to the left of the image of the house. "That's the twink. That's the master." I said I assumed the red color going up the middle of the image of himself was kundalini. Jeremy took out his red crayon, making the kundalini strokes stronger, going upwards more, and also downward towards the foundationless house. I remarked that I thought it was interesting that the kundalini image was now coming out of where there seemed to be no foundation. Jeremy then grabbed a blue crayon and drew blue circles around the twink and the master images. He said, "I'm going to contain them, they're like bubbles. They're floating in a bubble." I said I was curious about how the image of him was situated between the images of master and twink. I asked him to tell me about that and the black color in the spaces in between.

For Jeremy the black was not supposed to be so dark, it just represented atmosphere. But when I asked if he might move some aspect of the drawing, Jeremy said, "When I'm thinking of being in, and looking at that dream at the back of that house, it seemed kind of dark." I asked Jeremy to move the most compelling aspect of the dream image, and he chose the red-colored kundalini. He stood and went to the middle of the room, letting his arms rise up from his sides and back down. I asked him to repeat the movement with some exaggeration to see if any images or insights arose from it. Jeremy said he was thinking about where the dream had gone after what he had initially shared with me. I asked him to elaborate on the rest of the dream.

As the first dream progressed into a different scene, Jeremy was again with a young twink and there was a house renovation project happening. But he mentioned that the house belonged to friends of his parents, Margaret and Fred. Jeremy had loved their house as a child. Jeremy went on to describe how in the dream, "I'm in the house and it's like they're clearing out the house of family members, because people have died, and I'm there with a 'twink' and they have already gotten most of the stuff out. I was there to look to see if there was anything I wanted of the stuff that was left. But then somehow I had to be involved in renovating it, and there was another foundation problem. I'm walking over on this one side of the room, and then realized that it dropped way down like this; it was a big and sloping and had cracks and things. So, it is another problem with the foundation on the backside of this house. And these people, they're involved in a little party after a death, where there's food and what not. We could have food, the twink and I, but we weren't really a part of this group at all. So we felt separated and not really part of the group. Nobody wanted to interact with us. We sat at our own little table away from the people."

Jeremy then clarified that this dream followed the first dream on the same night. I told him I was curious about where he drew the line of kundalini down into the foundationless house, that something felt evocative about the connection between the two images.

Jeremy began another movement exploration, using his hands to explore the space behind him and in front of him. Although he reported having more feeling in his body, he also expressed a sense of separateness and loneliness, and that related to the people in the dream who didn't want to sit with him and didn't seem to want him. He again reiterated that he really wanted to fix the foundation. I asked him what movement might be associated with fixing the foundation. He took a step to the side, saying "We would be over here," and while he was doing that movement he suddenly exclaimed, "Whoa, it drops way down! Oh my god! That really felt like I stepped really way down. I want to jack this up right here, jack it up, up! I want it to be level."

At that point I asked Jeremy to intensify the movement of his arms, which were lifting up, as if lifting up the foundation of the house. I asked him to slow down, and really feel into the movement. Jeremy went to rest on his knees, with his arms open at his sides, his head and neck tilted back. I asked Jeremy what images or emotions were coming up in this position. He said, "It's like I'm connected to the source and all the other party and people and everything. The source and the sense of it is like, 'Oh, I have this connection with Margaret.'"

"Margaret, your mother's friend?" I asked.

"I have had a connection with her off and on, like a guide or something."

"Kind of an older, feminine figure?" I asked. I reminded him that he had said previously that she was always in a good mood and that she was good-spirited. Jeremy seemed in his own space and deeply engaged with the movement and the dream images. He murmured, "Right, and I really want to fix the house." He then got on the floor on his hands and knees, rocking back and forth a little bit. He reiterated, "I want to fix that fricking house and get it back to its normal self."

At this point Jeremy came out of the movement and took a moment to refresh himself. When he came back he requested some water. I asked him how he was feeling now. "I still feel all the shakti in me and around me, but I feel more grounded somehow. It's really strange. I'm surprised, I feel more grounded than I did when I first came in." I remarked that he did appear to be quieter, more at peace.

I asked him if he felt complete with the movement and drawing, and if there was anything else he wanted to share about kundalini or the dream, and he said yes. Jeremy did share that in his work life he had become much calmer and less reactive to difficult clients, particularly after his time on retreat in India, and that it felt like a big shift for him, and he was extremely grateful for that.

We wound down the interview and agreed to meet the following month.

The Second Interview

I began the second interview with Jeremy by asking him if anything came up for him right after our interview or later that might be related to our talk or the drawings. Jeremy said that soon after our interview, while he was sitting in meditation class, he had the sensation that he could change gravity. I wasn't clear on what he meant by that, and I asked him to explain further.

Jeremy said, "So I was in class and I was just getting a sense in the shakti that anything was possible and I would feel this lightning feeling of, 'Oh, this could, if you look really deep, you could see this could happen.' I was noticing that also in my meditation at home for a little bit, then I just looked over at that drawing, and I was like, 'Oh! Underneath, it almost looked like the last thing I draw in there.'" Jeremy pointed to his first drawing. "It's almost like a little rocket going off and I'm in my seat. The house doesn't really have much foundation, so it is kind of floating. So it was funny that that just struck me. It's like, 'Oh, it's funny that this would come coincidentally after I drew that picture.' Because I wasn't thinking about that particular thing at all from the dream or the picture."

Jeremy had put his drawing from our interview in his meditation space, so when he was meditating he could glance at it, and he'd also see it every day when he sat to meditate. I remembered back to our first interview together when he mentioned the upside-down pendulum in his body, with the round part at the top, and the stem of the pendulum going downward to his first chakra. I imagined there was a connection or resonance with that experience and his sense of the possibility of changing gravity, in addition to his reference to the shakti in his drawing being like a "rocket going off," with its propulsion hurtling him above his house.

Jeremy acknowledged what I said but moved on swiftly to another dream he had after our first interview. "I was on a plane and it needed to land but the runway is destroyed. So the plane has to land in a gravel-type area where there is no tarmac. Nathaji and people from the practice are on the plane. I'm sitting backwards for some reason and we are almost touching down and I realize I don't have my seat belt. I'm struggling with it to get it on and can't, and I say, 'I can't get it on,' and Nathaji just says, 'We've already landed.' I was expecting a lot of bumping and was afraid I'd get thrown all around, but I didn't. I didn't feel the touchdown, it was so smooth."

Jeremy had many dreams that he wrote down during the month between our first interview and the second. He flipped through his journal and started reading them to me. Another house dream came up that seemed particularly archetypal. Jeremy read, "I had a dream about being in a house in a big storm. The house was on top of a hill, but waves of the ocean were coming up not far away. The ocean had risen, like global warming. I realized the house down from me was flooded. Mark from high school and Richard, Richard is the person I had sex with in high school, had houses nearby. Then somehow I got into the little village. It seemed like there was flooding everywhere. Richard knew a tunnel that would take us to see if some other people lower down the hill were all right. There were four of us with a flashlight descending steps. I worried that the floodwaters would suddenly come up in the tunnel and drown us. Later, the dream seemed focused on the Airbnb in my house downstairs and neighbors. There was a going back and forth to see each other's places. I tried to reach someone but I didn't have their number, then the realization that the foundation of the house next door was deteriorated and there were gaps in the concrete. It's interesting because that's the same—this foundation stuff."

As Jeremy read his dreams aloud, he began seeing his own themes and trends in the dreams that he hadn't noticed before. He then related a few similar snippets of dreams with the theme of overflowing toilets and showers with potentially dirty water in them. Then he relayed a final dream from this period that we chose to work with in more depth. The location of the dream was in Michigan, in a town close to where Jeremy grew up.

He read the dream from his journal. "So I was in Sheraton, Michigan, with two other people in a home of one other person's grandfather, who died, and looking at all the old stuff in the house, and all of a sudden, there was this overwhelming feeling of loving kindness that filled me and nearly knocked me down to the floor. I was unable to speak for a few minutes. One of the other people said they felt their grandfather's presence. Then the dream changed to having some angry entity that suddenly found me and got inside me. It was a spirit that needed to keep moving on, but it was difficult to get it to go. It went on and on in this dream with me waking up because my body was uncomfortable and going right back into the dream. In the dream, I was just getting exhausted. I actually was getting exhausted because I kept waking up and my body hurt and the whole thing was exhausting. I woke up and I didn't feel very rested. But I was in this church thing, this balcony, and the entity was drowning, pulling down my energy. [A female friend] said we needed to crawl down this little corridor and I really just wanted to rid myself of the angry entity."

I asked Jeremy to close his eyes and feel into the grandfather image and the emotion of loving-kindness. Jeremy tried to feel into the sense of loving-kindness, but didn't feel that so much as a sense of spaciousness. While he continued to feel that spaciousness, he could at the same time see the face of the angry entity. The entity, Jeremy said, seemed to be saying, "You might be able to hold it off for now, but I'll get you later." This made Jeremy sad. I asked him to describe the face a bit more and he said it had a big jaw, and a loud mouth. Jeremy began to feel uncomfortable and moved to the floor. I reminded him that he could open his eyes and look around the room to get out of the feeling at any time. He reported he was beginning to feel a lot of sadness. Jeremy said, "It's like all those dreams, the sewer, and all those places just reminded me of that, or the going through the tunnel, the fear of the worry that the water's going to come and drown me."

I asked Jeremy if he would like to draw any of the images and he chose the grandfather. When he was done, Jeremy named the image "Loving Grandfather."

Loving Grandfather

Jeremy noticed that his image didn't look very old. Grandfather was in a house with a blue chair and a fireplace, and there were photos and pictures on the wall. The evil entity was not in the picture, and I asked Jeremy if he would like to draw that image separately. He agreed.

Bully Trump

As we worked with this image, Jeremy eventually named it "Bully Trump." I asked him about the qualities of this image. Jeremy said, "It's like chaos creating chaos." I put Bully Trump next to Loving Grandfather. I asked Jeremy to notice the different qualities of energy between the two. He still felt the spacious energy when he looked at the grandfather image, and that the grandfather felt more powerful than all the chaos of the Bully Trump image. He felt that even though this entity was chaotic, and a bully, he still had compassion for him—even if he was bad, he was mostly just hurting himself. He related it to a movie in which one man loved another man but could not express his love. When the character in the movie attempts to express himself, it comes out as rage, and the character burned the house down of the man he loved. Jeremy just felt sorry for that character, rather than angry or hateful towards him.

We were coming to the close of our interview, and I asked Jeremy to take the pictures home with him so he could move the images or do more drawing if he wanted to. I also suggested he could do dialogues between the two images. I sensed some resistance from Jeremy in doing that, and I reassured him he didn't have to do it.

In an interesting coincidence for our process, Jeremy was going back to Michigan in the next month to visit his mother. I thought it seemed synchronistic to our work together on his dreams about homes from childhood and his hometown. It was hard to say with certainty if the dreams were a result of knowing he was going to take a trip, or if he decided to take a trip out of an unconscious urge from his dreams. We agreed to meet when he returned in late August or early September.

The Third interview

Jeremy and I met for our final interview two months after our second interview. Jeremy started the interview by telling me about his trip to Michigan. Jeremy recalled, "When I went back to Michigan, surprisingly enough, I felt like I was coming home in some ways that I hadn't expected at all." He said he hadn't felt that sense of homecoming on other visits to his family in Michigan. This time, he had visited with his ex-wife and had a fabulous time. They went to Drummond Island, which held special significance for him for its beauty and peacefulness. In fact, in an unexpected move, he bought a small house on the island while there on his visit. I was surprised at this news from Jeremy, but somehow felt it was a very significant decision on his part, and that it might have been initiated consciously or unconsciously by his deeper psyche that revealed itself in his dreams.

Jeremy had not done any journaling or moved the dream drawing from the first interview, but he had kept a record of his dreams. He is a prolific dreamer and he read many dreams to me. Thematically, many of the dreams were about houses. Some of the houses were flooded, and some needed renovation. Then there were a series of dreams in which houses were on fire or burned. Jeremy read the first one to me. "I had to go down this windy road. There was a fire on the road and I was looking at property first and seeing homes that had been burnt by fire. One home was having a party for an unrelated group of people. The people were downstairs. It was kind of like using it for a retreat or something. The owners were upstairs. I went up and they told me about the fire and where it burned."

I asked Jeremy how he felt in that dream. He said he didn't recall, but he then said that in the next segment of the dream he was a young kid playing in a house that was partially burned. Then Jeremy realized that there were a lot of houses burning in his dreams, saying that he didn't like burned houses, or fires. Jeremy observed that in many of his dreams he was younger than his current age, either a young teen or in his early twenties. He remarked that those were difficult years for him.

He rapidly turned to another dream to illustrate his point of the difficult years. "My family is having a party with friends. First my mother pours or spills food on me and I changed my clothes. Then my dad is trying to open a salsa container or something and he's been drinking and he spills it all over my face and shirt. I start screaming, 'Where are the grownups here? What do you think it's like being a young kid with no adults?' Then the dream seems to change. I'm in and out of sleep and all I remember is fires. God!"

Many of Jeremy's dreams don't seem to connect directly to kundalini, but they certainly have archetypal themes, which I'll explore in the reflections section of this chapter. Yet, there was a sense that kundalini was integral as almost a background to what was appearing in Jeremy's dream life. I brought the conversation back to kundalini, and asked Jeremy if during these dreams or even during his time in Michigan, he'd felt a significant presence of kundalini. He replied, "There are times I've been feeling really still, more still." I asked him how that translated or was incorporated into his everyday life. "I feel it sometimes just doing things. Like the whole time I was in Michigan, I just felt it, whatever we were doing, I could feel that place inside."

Jeremy mentioned that his ex-wife really noticed a change in him. She noticed that he was "more content and not stressed about stuff." I asked him if there was anything else he noticed about his dreams or kundalini, or the process of the interviews we did together. Jeremy said thoughtfully, "It seems like maybe the shakti—maybe there's a way that some of this is weaving some kind of healing into my past. There's something being reworked with all this young stuff. That one dream of them spilling something on me and where are the parents? It's like, yeah, that was my childhood. Where are the parents?"

Jeremy returned to thinking about the house he just bought. He felt it was significant in some way. Maybe he would not have it forever, but he felt he was supposed to be there now. There was something about Drummond Island that felt really powerful to him, and he recalled he had felt that way about the place since his childhood. I suggested we bring the interview to a close if he was ready. He said he was, but he pointed to his heart and said, "This place in here, there's still some healing stuff in this area that is happening. It seems tied to all that old stuff, all those dreams and things. I just forgot about the dreams, but when I read them here, I'm like 'oh wow.' And then they all come back."

Jeremy's statement was a tender insight, and I felt pleased for him that he recognized there was some healing to do based on the work he had already done. There is transformative power in being able to view dreams and drawings objectively, outside of one's own mind, that creates a space to see more clearly what is happening in the psyche. I felt gratitude for Jeremy's candidness and his willingness to share very personal and often painful memories with me. We ended our interview time together, feeling it was complete.

Reflections on Jeremy's Story

In this interview series, though Jeremy and I talked about kundalini, the experience of kundalini itself seemed to get subsumed by the archetypal energy of the complexes in the psyche. When I attempted to steer the conversation back to kundalini, Jeremy's dreams and active imagination sessions through movement and drawing pointed repeatedly to what needed to be healed. Perhaps this was not surprising since the nature of Jeremy's major encounter with kundalini was brought about by a traumatic experience. Jeremy's sense of ego-self began to disintegrate as he surrendered his will and physical body to a master. This event appeared to be a physical enactment of the oppositional forces of twink and master in Jeremy's psyche. The complex that remained unconscious in the psyche was being played out externally.

The oppositional forces at work in Jeremy's psyche were between the energy of the twink, and the bullying, dominating energy of the master. The master energy may be considered the part of the psyche that acts as a defense mechanism to protect the rest of the psyche, as described previously in the work of Donald Kalsched in Colleen's story. If so, then what is apparent is a complex of opposites trying to reach resolution or integration, but the bullying energy in the psyche is thwarting the process. As this complex was projected outwards, Jeremy found himself in a very difficult and painful position both physically and psychologically.

The first drawing Jeremy did showed in image-form this psychological dynamic playing out in the psyche—a twink is on one side of the drawing, and the master is on the other. Jeremy is floating over a house and the kundalini is running from beneath the broken foundation, through the house, and through his body. Jeremy had contained the energy of the master and twink within bubbles, almost as if to subdue the force of their energy, and then he reinforced the line of red kundalini a few times with the red crayon, as if to make that force stronger, perhaps to protect him.

Jeremy was also aware that he had projected his need to feel the opening and love in his heart onto romantic relationships, and the withdrawing of the projection was a relief to him. The focus could now be on his own heart and his connection with a numinous source—he didn't feel he needed to be dependent on another to connect to that sense of open-heartedness and love. His own work with kundalini and the shakti transmission offered in class strengthened this insight and kept him working in his meditation practice.

The repeating images of houses with missing or damaged foundations, houses being burned or flooded, and houses where he is present but not particularly welcome, is a very strong archetypal image throughout Jeremy's dreams. In the first interview and movement exercises, Jeremy could feel the sense of the foundation dropping "way down, and wanting to fix the foundation, to make it level." I suggest Jeremy had the sense of falling into a deeper layer of the psyche, closer to the unconscious, and the urge was to get balanced. In fact, this dream is reminiscent of Jung's own dream of a house he described in his memoir *Memories, Dreams, Reflections*, in which he discovered several levels of the house, and related these to levels in the psyche, from conscious conception of the self, to deep layers of the collective psyche. Over and over in Jeremy's dreams and dream explorations, he wished to fix the foundation of the house. It's interesting that after the first interview and movement exploration, Jeremy noted that he felt "more grounded"—an apt phrase to use considering he felt the foundation of his house image was broken. The movement exploration may have helped "level" some of that foundation by getting in touch with and moving the energy of the psyche.

We get a hint as to the origins of the damage to the foundation in the later dream with his parents. Although Jeremy and I did not explore the history of his family dynamics, in one dream both his parents by turn dumped food on him, making him dirty. His father was drinking alcohol in the dream, and Jeremy stated that he felt more like the caretaker than the taken care of as a child. This might cause something to feel foundationally missing in his psychological development or sense of love and safety. At the same time, he did receive support and nurturance from close neighbors. An important childhood support figure, Margaret, showed up in one of Jeremy's house dreams as a positive wise old woman figure that gave him comfort and stability. Similarly, in the second interview we explored the loving grandfather, a wise old man archetypal image. These two strong, archetypal images from the unconscious appear to be supportive images of love and wholeness. The grandfather is a powerful image of loving-kindness for Jeremy, and yet as he was blissfully overwhelmed with a profound feeling of loving-kindness in the dream, the image of "Bully-Trump" comes in and pulls his energy down, as if drowning him.

Referring again to Kalsched's work with trauma, we can observe how this bullying part of the psyche seems to be self-protecting against the benevolent energy of the loving grandfather. One might also view the Bully Trump image as connected to the similar energy as the Master that Jeremy had initially sought out. It would appear that a complex that had played out externally in the world was still appearing in his psyche through the energetic polarities of Loving Grandfather and Bully Trump. I would suspect too, that growing up gay in a time and culture that was not overtly supportive of homosexuality would be a further destabilizing factor in Jeremy's early life experiences. This is hinted at in the dreams where he is with a twink at parties in houses, but they are not truly welcome or part of the group, and end up at their own table, feeling isolated.

It is notable that Jeremy felt more at home when he returned to his hometown during the summer when we conducted the interviews. The numinous and archetypal quality of his relationship with Drummond Island motivated him to unexpectedly buy a house there. In Jungian psychology the house in dreams typically symbolizes the psyche, with many potential layers, from personal to collective. For Jeremy, it may be that the archetypal energy in the image of the house was being projected outwardly onto a house in a spiritually numinous place from his childhood, but the projection had a positive feeling-tone to it. Perhaps returning again and again to that place will be healing to the parts of Jeremy that are still wounded.

In reflecting on Jeremy's story, it seemed necessary to first address the psychological and archetypal components that appear in his interviews, dreams, and movement explorations. But what role did kundalini play in Jeremy's experiences? At first kundalini seemed to be in the background, something separate from the experiences and stories that unfolded during our time together. But reviewing our interviews, I remembered how Jeremy experienced the energy of kundalini becoming stronger with the intensity of emotional affect, and as I looked at the drawings, it occurred to me that kundalini was playing an essential role, much like Jung's concept of the transcendent function, much like it did with Ryan's process.

The transcendent function is a Jungian theory and process where the oppositional clashes between the conscious and unconscious psyche are mediated by a transcendent third, something new that arises between them, what Jung called "a living birth that leads to a new level of being, a new situation." This third thing that arises is felt as alive and full of psychic energy.

We can see that in Jeremy's moment of crisis in the hands of the master, his conscious ego position weakened considerably, and coupled with being drugged, the energetic force of kundalini was unleashed. Perhaps it was not yet acting as a transcendent function, but rather as energy released in the body-mind system from the unconscious. Since I have heard anecdotally from others, and also experienced firsthand the eruption of kundalini when the ego loses its dominant position in the psyche, it may be that the power of kundalini normally remains dormant in the unconscious. When the door to the unconscious is opened, particularly when this occurs involuntarily, many archetypal images may emerge, and even beyond images, the energy of the images themselves may burst forth. I am suggesting that energy is kundalini.

If understood properly and worked with in balance with the conscious psyche, I further suggest, as in the case of Jeremy, the kundalini acts as a supportive energetic force that mediates the conscious and unconscious boundaries. In Jeremy's case, as we explored dreams in movement, the kundalini energy arose and increased in strength in tandem with the quantity of emotional energy present. These moments reinforced my sense that for Jeremy, the energy of kundalini was acting as a healing elixir, becoming more potent when the emotions became more pronounced—even emotions such as sadness, as if the kundalini energy and the emotion were intertwined. Jeremy had the insight that the kundalini "is weaving some healing into my past." Though the past events cannot be changed, healing them over time with the energy of kundalini and conscious awareness is possible.

I believe this was the case for Jeremy, not in his first encounter, but as he worked consciously with the energy over time. Kundalini helped Jeremy confront and work through past wounds. Kundalini may be considered the process of the transcendent function and also the transcendent function itself, arising out of what initially felt like an impossibly painful situation. This energy continued as both a healing energy to old wounds, and as a palpably felt mediating energy bringing the conscious mind into dialogue with unconscious material within the vessel of the body-mind system, furthering the process of transformation and individuation over time.

CHAPTER EIGHT

Maria's Story: Navigating Subjective and Objective Experience

Maria is a woman in her late 50s who has the kind of youthful energy that allows her to ride her bike up the East Coast of the United States for a summer holiday, travel to India for a month, and then land in Spain the following month to sip cappuccino in the piazzas. She's been a television journalist, a yoga instructor, a therapist, and when I interviewed her, she was taking classes in business school. She's an artist with a creative bent towards life in general, and she approaches her spiritual life with an open-ended curiosity.

I've known Maria for about ten years. We met when she started coming to kundalini meditation classes. We have also roomed together on numerous retreats, most recently in Ganeshpuri, India, where we bonded over impossibly complicated mosquito netting, broken plumbing, cold showers, mysterious stomach ailments, and the magic of walking to Nityananda's shrine at 4:00 a.m. to meditate.

I asked Maria to participate in my research study because of her open-minded approach to spiritual experiences, her connection to kundalini energy, and her ability to express herself in images. I was at ease interviewing Maria, but I had no preconceived ideas of what might transpire during our time together.

The First Interview

To open our dialogue, I asked Maria if she would like to relate a specific kundalini experience happening for her now, or one that had happened in the past. Maria chose an experience in the recent past for her, one that had transpired the prior week, but which was still unfolding for her in the present. Maria described sitting in meditation class, feeling the energy of shakti-kundalini pouring into the top of her head, but also the sensation of the kundalini energy from inside her rising out of the top of her head simultaneously.

This was a fairly regular experience for Maria in class. But on this particular night the experience unfolded further. Maria described it as "like I had an orgasm in my head. It's hard to explain, but it just felt like my brain/head was melting, and it felt orgasmically delicious and it was located in my head." I asked Maria if she had any images associated with the experience and she said she didn't, but afterwards, even days afterwards, she felt a sense of "coming into stillness, like a field of stillness." And she said that this sense of stillness drew her attention to it, and she wanted to be immersed in it. She noticed that just thinking about the experience facilitated the experience of pulsing energy in her head, even as we were talking in the interview. Maria closed her eyes for a moment, tuning into the subtle sensations. With her eyes still closed, she reported, "What I actually am noticing is that when I put my attention outwardly, I feel irritated. This is so interesting because I'm just noticing that this has been happening."

When Maria's attention was focused inwardly, and centered in her heart space, everything felt "peaceful and soothing and calming." But when she opened her eyes and focused outwardly, she felt it was "very irritating," and this dichotomy of experience was curious to her. She then related several other incidences when meditating or getting energetic healing work done that she also had the sensation of a calm and peaceful interiority; when she had to engage with the exterior world, she felt irritation in having to leave the subjective, peaceful state. She felt it was both difficult and somewhat aggravating to leave that calm, heart-centered place.

Maria offered an example of this experience. "It's like when we're deep in meditation and we come out and somebody immediately starts talking to us. There's a different level of our personality that has to pull out. That file has to open and we have to come out and interact, but there's this other part that's like, 'I'm here, I want to hang out here, I don't want to do that.'"

Maria clearly expressed the distinctions between the subjective and objective experience, so I suggested she take some time to draw the experiences. I asked her to first get centered in the subjective experience and gave her about twenty minutes to draw from that space. Then I asked her to take twenty minutes to draw from the experience of being pulled outwards into the exterior world. These images were the result of her two drawing explorations.

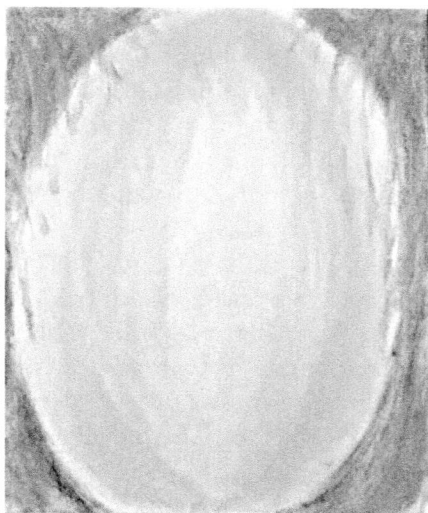

The Purity

Pre-Integration

When Maria finished with these drawings, she exclaimed, "It felt so good to do that. Oh my god. I can't even believe it. It's incredible. How wonderful to receive!" It seemed a relief for Maria to get the images out and onto paper. What became apparent to me was that the central image of an oval colored in gold stayed relatively intact from drawing to drawing, but there was a definite sense of discord in the second drawing, with the frazzled strokes of color of blue, red, green, and black coming out from the center, which seemed smaller on the page than in the first drawing. In my subjective experience, the first drawing felt soothing with its upward flow and a slight glow that gave me an overall feeling of harmony. In the second drawing, I felt a palpable sense of stress.

I suggested Maria put the two drawings side by side so that we could explore them through movement. Maria stood by her first drawing, arms overhead, and then she brought them down in a circular motion, while arching her back and head backwards. She brought her hands to the space around her head and neck, as if feeling the space around that part of her body, and then she made a scooping motion from her pelvic area upwards to the area of her heart. I had her repeat that motion several times so she could notice what images or emotions arose with the movement. Maria shared that when her hands were by her pelvis she felt some fear, but when her hands reached her head there was a sense of "deliciousness."

While Maria was moving, I felt the shakti-kundalini in the room. It was a feeling of pulsation, similar to how one might feel an energy current running through a cable. In this case it seemed to fill the room, and I could also feel the pulsation in my own head. I suggested that Maria engage her second drawing in a movement exploration while staying connected to her heart.

Maria's movements differed with the second drawing. One had hovered over the crown of her head, and one was positioned in front of her forehead. I asked Maria how it felt to be in that position. "This is really powerful. It feels like these parts are coming in from the outside and penetrating me. This physical position feels protective. It's like a process that's happening that needs to be protected and I feel really vulnerable when I do this."

I asked her to move back and forth between the drawings, letting herself express the drawings in movement, creating a movement dialogue between the two images. Maria noticed that as she moved between the two drawings she was "trying to understand how to integrate this energy into this experience." I suggested that she let the movement do the integrative work for her. She shifted between the movement of her first drawing and the movement expressed with her second drawing. Organically, a third movement spontaneously developed, with Maria rocking her hips back and forth with slightly bent knees. She began to bring the lower body movement together with her arms and hands raised above her head, and then gently float downwards, palms facing away from her body, and then back up to over her head with her palms facing up. Her breath deepened. When I asked her what she was feeling, she said she noticed some fear when her palms were facing outwards, and when they were rising up if felt more comforting and loving. I suggested that she keep rocking her hips but play with the palms outwards and the palms facing inwards towards her. "Wow," Maria exclaimed. I asked her what she was noticing. "There's a lot of energy here. Instead of fear, it feels more like resistance of this huge flow of energy. It's overwhelming me."

I asked her where it felt safe in her body and she gestured towards her heart. She then went into a squatting position. I asked her how that felt and she said if felt great, like it was releasing caught up or crunched up energy. Maria then began to twist at the waist side to side, which also felt like a release for her. I told her I was curious how the rocking of her lower body and the twisting felt compared to the upper arm movements she had been doing. "It's feels very clearing and maybe more balanced. I can feel it more in my entire system—more integrated." I told her I noticed that with her feet splayed and her hands at her sides, she appeared to be in a more powerful position. I asked her to name the drawings.

"I would name the first one 'The Purity' and the second one 'Pre-Integration.'"

I asked Maria how she was feeling after the drawing and movement exploration. She responded, "I feel great. I feel really centered in my heart. What's that word when you bring something from the outside inside?"

"Incorporated?" I suggested. Maria seemed to like that word, but she was still searching for a better one.

"Absorbed?" I offered.

"Yeah, absorbed or inverted. That's a really powerful image for me. I feel more seated in that. It's as if I'm a little tiny speck sitting inside of that." I reviewed parts of the experience that Maria had related to me, to see if I had captured it correctly, which prompted her to elaborate more fully on her experience.

"It was more like how to sit in that space while the world is happening around me and how to be really seated there without being pulled out of it into whatever is happening over here and how to, instead, allow that energy pulling me out and integrate it into this, what's happening here. When I do that, that's when that explosion sound, like that huge amount of energy opened up for me in that second drawing and I don't have to resist this, I can take it and be with it, integrate it, and transform it, and bring it into here."

Maria and I both observed that her last movements were more firmly planted on the ground and solid, which felt satisfying, and a good place to end our first interview.

The Second Interview

Our second interview started by reviewing our first interview together, and noticing any developments that had occurred over the six weeks between them. Maria noticed a general trend towards more open-heartedness, and an equanimity that was less likely to be disturbed by outside events. She said that she felt more integrated with the internal and external spheres of her life, and she was more grounded and centered. Maria had recorded a few dreams during the interim of our interviews, and we turned our conversation towards those.

In the first dream, Maria walked into a big place with religious Christian iconography of Jesus and the Virgin Mary on the walls. In her dream Maria asked what the place was, and was told it was "The Institute for Awakening the Third Eye." I asked her how she felt about the name. Maria said she "was kind of astonished, like wow, this is what this place is. It was cool." Since it was such a brief dream, she didn't have much more to say about it.

In the second dream she was in a house and the roof was caving in. I asked her to feel where that "roof caving in" image might be in her body. She said she felt it at the crown of her head, like a "hole in the top of my head. I have this sense of blackness or space, emptiness. It's that sense of folding in on itself." I inquired about the emotional resonance she might feel accompanying this image and Maria said it felt like spaciousness, and that it was very quiet and peaceful, as well as feeling limitless. I asked her how she felt now, feeling deeper into that space. Maria described it as feeling "very loving, like a deep lovingness."

I had Maria stay with the physical, emotional, and energetic resonance of the dream image that was located at the top of her head to see if it had any more information that it might reveal. That space felt bigger than her body, she said, "more like a portal" that felt connected to her heart. It was difficult for her to feel into the experience physically because somehow that felt "off." The portal at the top of her head was connected to her heart, but it didn't feel like a linear connection.

I then asked Maria if she could bring the two dreams together, to overlap them like pieces of tissue paper and see what that might feel like. She went with this idea easily and said she could feel a pulsation and excitement associated with the dream of The Institute for the Awakening of the Third Eye. She said she could feel the pulsation of the first dream within the area of the portal of the second dream.

I asked her to draw an image of the pulsation and the portal together, because I was curious if that image would trigger further insights or information. I had the sense that Maria, being an artist, put a lot of energy in her drawings, maybe more so than in her spoken word. This is the image that arose from Maria's dreams.

Pulsation and Portal

I invited her to tell me about the drawing. She pointed to the small circle at the bottom of the picture with just a touch of pink at its center. "This is like the heart, this connection between the head or the third eye and the heart connection." She pointed back and forth from the smaller circle to the larger black circle swirling above it. The larger circle was the head or third eye portal. She described the blue, green, and yellow spurting from the portal as "just space that's coming out of there, it's expressing itself." She felt there was something really satisfying in creating the drawing. I asked her to spend time over the next month to continue to move and draw from this one drawing, to elaborate on it along with any journaling she wanted to do. Maria expressed again how much she enjoyed doing the process of checking in with her body, still or in movement, and also doing the drawing. She said, "I love this and then I forget how much I love it and then I do it and I'm like, 'Oh my god, I love it! Why am I not doing this all the time? It's so cool!'" We ended the session on that note, and I looked forward to seeing how the work with Maria would evolve in the next month.

The Third Interview

During our last interview six weeks later, Maria and I again focused our attention on her dreams. She had three short dreams in close succession that are thematically similar and seem to relate to her spiritual life.

In the first dream, Maria was in a room with many other people. Suddenly, she noticed Nathaji, our spiritual teacher, walk through the room with a couple of other teachers. She said, "I don't know if these teachers were from our practice or from some other practice, but they came walking through, and it was like they were invisible, like nobody else could see them but me." She said she felt fine about it and decided to go with them. Describing the dream further, Maria said, "It was like walking through time and space. It was like they were the crack in the space and time and I was joining them." She said that in the dream it felt amazing and magical, and that it felt "purposeful and very right." When I asked her to explain more fully what the "feeling right" experience was, she said, "It's like the levels of reality. We have this every day. Our everyday is like one level of reality, but then there are many different levels of reality happening all the time, and then there's a psychic reality."

Maria's second dream was also short. In it she said she "received a huge amount of energy that I experienced moving through my body and through the top of my head. It's like my head is blown off from the energy." In the dream Maria remembered just allowing the energy to be there and relaxing into it.

Maria's third dream came to her like a revelation. She read her journal entry to me. "I'm in space and it is revealed to me that this space is conscious, deep, and alive. And then it's revealed that there are other deeper dimensions that I am only able to catch a glimpse of, and they're revealed in space waves—alive, conscious dimensions."

In this dream Maria felt both in the experience and the receiver of a revelation. The understanding in the dream was that though it was space, which we don't normally think of as conscious, there was "another layer of space, like another dimension, and then there was even another dimension. It was consciousness. It looked like space but it was actually consciousness." The dream left Maria feeling awestruck.

After these three dreams that occurred over no longer than a week, Maria reported that she hadn't been dreaming much, but she did feel that there was an integration happening inside her. The sense of peace had deepened, and there was also a sense of longing for it in everything. I remarked that this sense of longing to stay in that peace reminded me of our first interview together, with the drawings of the inner state and the irritation of being pulled outwards. She agreed that it was similar, and that if she was out of the peaceful state it felt "super exhausting." It was as if the way she had conducted her life up until that point was no longer sustainable going forward. I asked Maria what external changes had been made to accommodate staying in the more peaceful state. She replied that she stayed "in the flow" without fighting it. She said, "I don't have to do those silly little things that we find like, 'Oh I have to go run this errand.' No, not really, I really don't."

Maria also told me that her work life was shifting more dramatically. As a therapist she had decided not to take on any new clients. She felt like it wasn't "reviving," so she was in the process of letting it go. On the other hand, she had a creative idea for a software app, so she was taking business classes to see how she could create it and launch it. Again, Maria felt like the idea for the software application was just flowing through her and she was allowing it to do so.

We turned our conversation to a drawing she had done during the previous month.

Space and Light

Maria was less satisfied with this drawing aesthetically. She felt it didn't quite convey the stillness she felt inside. However, she pointed to the black, bold lines and said that they represented space. "That's how I feel internally, I guess. Space and then this light energy that's coming, that's there. It's not coming anywhere, it's just there." In the center of the drawing there is an inverted triangle in yellow and white. I told Maria I noticed that the colors were similar as her previous drawings, although differently configured in this one. She agreed, saying it was just coming from a different perspective. She again mentioned that what was happening for her now was a continued integration of these energetic experiences, both from meditation and from her dreams. One aspect of this integration was a strong feeling of gratitude for her life. There was now a feeling of wholeness to her life that had arisen gradually, over time. The experience of the brain orgasm and energetic releases were a part of that overall process. For Maria, the spiritual work with kundalini in her life was felt like an "incredible, deep, rich unfolding."

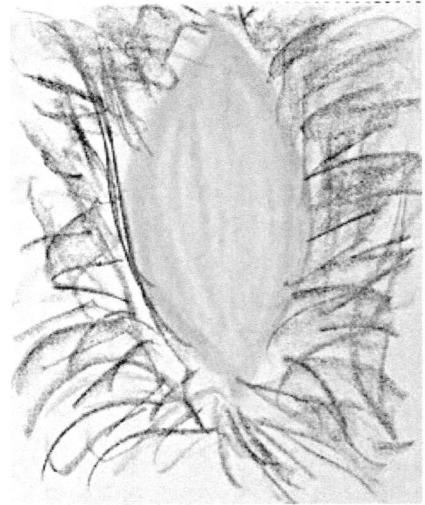

Reflections on Maria's Story

In Jung's work on psychology and alchemy he contended that insight occurs not in the mind or in the body, but in a place between the two which consists of a more subtle reality that can only be expressed symbolically, in image. In Maria's artwork, particularly the first drawings of what appears to be an egg, that palpable, living image represented experience that was not easily summed up verbally.

For Maria, the egg-shaped image was the experience of her internal space, which resonated with a sense of stillness. We can also see, especially in the color version, that it had a glowing quality to it. The image seemed to me to be a container of that internalized, quiet self, a place where she enjoyed dwelling. Maria herself did not refer to the image as an egg, but it seemed to hold that significance to me when I looked at it.

Maria descried her experience moving both the "Purity" image and the "Pre-Integration" image. "It was as if I'm a little tiny speck sitting inside of that." She experienced herself as the consciousness, or sentient being inside the vessel of the egg. There was a resonance of gestation, of not wanting to engage in the outside world while she was attempting to stay within the quiet stillness that the experience of her brain melting into orgasmic bliss ushered in. She realized through her movement exploration that she was both pushing away distracting environmental stimuli that required her to engage life at the level of persona or ego, and she was also pushing away a tremendous amount of energy that she realized she was slightly afraid of. But when she worked with the external energy instead of resisting it, she felt a huge explosion of energy.

Kundalini, too, is symbolically referenced and phenomenologically experienced as a flash of lightning. It can be felt as a flash coming in from above as the descent of shakti, or as coming up from below as kundalini rises from the base of the spine towards the top of the head. Although this may happen with varying degrees of intensity over time, the experience is spontaneous and autonomous, and often quite powerful. For Maria, it was when she stopped resisting both the external energy and the sense of powerful internal flow that she had a flash of insight— the insight that she was resisting the flow of energy because it seemed overwhelming—and then she became conscious, centered, and grounded with the powerful energy moving through her.

In our second interview the process of integration continued, resulting in Maria feeling more openhearted and able to engage the regular demands of external life with more equanimity. She also reported several dreams with archetypal images. In the first dream there are religious images from the Christian and Eastern traditions: Jesus, Mary, and the Third Eye Institute. This dream seems to portend the future, as she is in a place of learning, and the process is one of awakening. What might be awakening is indicated by the iconic sacred images on the wall—something numinous seemed to be manifesting. The Third Eye Institute may also be symbolic of the transcendent function which I discussed in Jeremy's chapter.

In the second dream Maria reported the top of her head was like a "roof caving in," and that this caving in created a portal to cosmic space at the top of her head, traditionally the place in Eastern energy practices known as the crown chakra. The crown chakra is the doorway where the individualized sense of kundalini is merged with the larger sense of a cosmic reality. This is the location where the personalized sense of ego-self can dissolve into the larger sense of self as unbounded by the ego, the archetypal and cosmic self. As Maria drew this dream she could feel the heart space and the portal at the top of her head connected, "but not in a linear way." It seemed that there was an extension of herself in the grounded place of the heart, that nevertheless was beginning to simultaneously feel more universal rather than purely personal.

In our third interview together, the dream themes continued to unfold. Maria described three short dreams that came in a series of nights. In one, she is with Nathaji and other unknown spiritual teachers, and they are leading her through "a crack in time and space." She was entering a psychic space that was very different than everyday reality. The dream appeared to be revealing a dimension of psychic life beyond the personal or concretely material realms.

In the second dream, Maria was aware of a great deal of energy, the intense rush of shakti, coursing through her. The portal at the top of her head blew wide open from this energy, and she described it as her head blowing off. This seemed to be a transitional dream, a necessary widening of the portal to allow for her last dream to manifest, which is worth repeating here. "I'm in space and it is revealed to me that this space is conscious, deep, and alive. And then it's revealed that there are other deeper dimensions that I am only able to catch a glimpse of, and they're revealed in space waves—alive, conscious dimensions."

This dream was revelatory in nature. It indicated that the cosmos and other dimensions of reality were not dead or inert, but were conscious and alive.

Maria's dreams seemed to be moving beyond the personal psyche and into a multi-dimensional reality, and the vehicle or energy driving the progression of these dreams from personal to cosmic was the energy of shakti-kundalini.

Although Maria's dreams and experiences are extraordinary, how she integrated them over time was simply a matter of bringing her awareness to them and working with the energy, rather than resisting it. The transformation over time was subtle. From the shakti brain orgasm to dreams of the cosmos being fully alive and conscious, Maria's most significant psychological shift was experiencing a larger sense of gratitude for her life and a more profound experience of wholeness. This parallels the principle of individuation, which for Jung was the process of becoming psychologically whole and integrated, where unconscious psychic material is integrated with the conscious psyche. The movement towards wholeness continues throughout life and is not a one-time event. Working with conscious and unconscious material and the unification and integration of opposites over time is an organic process of the psyche that has awe-inspiring moments, but also moments of a quiet and profound sense of peace and connection with the universe. Experiences of kundalini can assist and underscore all of these potential human experiences.

CHAPTER NINE

Dana's Story:
Emergence of the Goddess

The story I will share about myself takes place during the time period between starting and finishing my dissertation, about 2014 to 2018. Though I've worked with kundalini energy for nearly 30 years, it was during the time of writing my dissertation that very unusual dreams began to happen. I will mainly reference my dreams to show progression, themes, sudden and unexpected turns in the path, and occasionally more questions that arose as I was conducting my research. In the stories of my co-researchers, there is the dialogic feel between the interviewer and interviewee. In my story, which lacks an objective interviewer, I will suggest possible interpretations of images and the psychological change and progression of my dreams. I will use the reflection to explore overarching themes, complexes, and synchronicities from a depth psychological perspective. Dreams can be interpreted in so many ways, and I have not used an outside facilitator or analyst to help decipher my dreams. So the dream interpretations will be my own, and without an outside facilitator may be incomplete. Yet the incompleteness may point to what remains in my unconscious, and you are welcome to your interpretations, which may offer something to your own process of thinking about kundalini and dreams.

The Beginning

In July of 2014 I was just beginning to formulate my research question. On July 8th I had the following dream:

I am at the library at Pacifica. I am searching in the library for books for a paper. I come upon a big white book the size of Jung's *The Red Book*, but it was white, and it said "kundalini," although I couldn't quite make out the word because it was interspersed with other letters. I could tell if I took the other letters out it said kundalini. Then I realized it must be in code, and it looked like kundalini was the same thing as alchemy—the pictures on the front of the book were alchemical symbols. I started to look at it differently, trying to pull out the extra letters to see what they said, but I was having a hard time doing it, and then I realized if I just looked at it like a white face with black letters (or looked at it like a black and white mirror image) I could figure out what it was, and it said the name of the author, which was "Boehme."

My unconscious psyche seemed to be onto something of my research topic before I consciously knew what I would research. In my opinion, kundalini is like alchemy because it is the transformation of consciousness on all levels of the psyche, immanent and transcendent. In the dream it was a matter of looking at kundalini differently that helped decipher the title. When I woke from this dream I remembered the name of Boehme, and though the name was familiar I could not consciously say who the historical figure of Boehme was. That sent me to an internet search, where I discovered that he was a German Christian mystic born in 1575. Boehme's spiritual visions began when he was an adolescent. One day while polishing a bowl, the light refracting from it mesmerized him. This somehow created a flash of transcendent, spiritual insight.

According to his conception of the cosmological order, God contained seven characteristics that were continuously facilitating interaction between cosmic unity and the diversity experienced in normal waking consciousness. The fourth characteristic caught my attention, because it is described as a flashing of fire. This image seemed analogous to kundalini, which can often be experienced as a flash of fire or light. This fourth stage for Boehme mediated between the coarse and harsh characteristics of the first three characteristics, and those of the more sublime characteristics of God in the higher characteristics. The interaction between all seven characteristics was not linear in its progression, but rather all characteristics intermingled in a kind of divine playfulness.

Boehme also considered God to have both male and female aspects in perfect harmony. The female aspect of God was Sophia, or divine wisdom. In Boehme's conception, Sophia was not a separate divinity outside of God nor a consort or partner of God, but rather was the feminine face of God. In Tantric tradition, kundalini is conceptualized as feminine, as Shakti, not different from divine consciousness, but as its power of manifestation. Kundalini within a person is the individuated expression of that divine consciousness, and as kundalini unfolds in the system and rises through the seven chakras, it weaves pure, unified divine consciousness into the fabric of individual consciousness.

My understanding and connection between the Boehme of my dream and the actual 16th century mystic of Boehme came much later. However, looking back on the dream, it appeared that elements of how kundalini unfolded in my own internal process throughout the dissertation writing was already seeded within the dream. In addition, there seemed to be a triadic correlation between kundalini, alchemy, and the mystic Boehme. What was remarkable to me beyond the personal nature of the dream was how either my unconscious, or the collective unconscious, retrieved a specific historical person to bring to the dream that I had no conscious recollection of knowing. Even more remarkable, this is not unique to me. Images of the collective unconscious make innumerable appearances in the dreams of people everywhere. It's almost as if the past is dropping hints to the future from a place where past and future are irrelevant. When we can work with these gifts of images, the potential for personal and collective understanding becomes more profound and meaningful.

The research and writing of the dissertation also seemed to parallel external events in my life, particularly in 2015. It was during that year that my spiritual teacher, Swami Khecaranatha, asked if I would like to become a teacher within our practice. This was a very serious offer and would require a tremendous personal commitment on my part. It involved quarterly retreats and trainings, service to the community, and eventually opening my own meditation center. In 2015 I was living in Jakarta, Indonesia, and so accepting to be a teacher required that I travel four times a year back to the United States to participate in the training. Regardless of the additional work and commitment, I felt it was the right path for me, and so my work with kundalini deepened during this time as my research for my dissertation also deepened.

Though consciously my research and writing of my literature review had an academic and mental tenor during this time, my dream life began to shift in unexpected ways that added an element of curiosity and surprise. Like water moving down a tributary and suddenly veering and creating a new conduit, my dreams began to suggest another branch of research that needed to be addressed in the dissertation. It began in November of 2015 while preparing to go on vacation with my husband to Myanmar. On November 8th, I had the following dream:

> I am at Rasa House and it is filled with witches. They're casually milling about doing some work here and there and talking—I think they're preparing for a ceremony or ritual. The head witch is putting my hair up in some kind of hairdo. I'm looking around thinking, "Okay, I guess I'm part of this tribe, I belong with the witches and that's not so bad or scary."

Rasa House, as I described earlier in Colleen's story, is the name of our cabin in the foothills of the Sierras. It is my retreat place where I go for relaxation, introspection, and peace. I was curious that witches had filled it in my dream, and that I was part of their tribe. The day before leaving for Myanmar I dreamed of being on the edge of an ocean with my husband and a big wave was coming in. And although it was large, there was a strong sense of being told in the dream that I was not to worry, I would be able to surf the wave even though it seemed huge. The dream itself felt very peaceful.

Myanmar is a stunning country, particularly outside of the busy cities. The countryside felt saturated in an atmosphere of something almost electric—like a humming aliveness permeating the space that surpassed the visual flora and fauna, or even the thousands of stupas pebbling the landscape. I pondered whether, in this Buddhist land that incorporated its animist spiritual roots, devotion to the divine in many forms animated the landscape in the same manner that James Hillman felt the Greek mythological tradition animated parts of Europe. The atmosphere felt lush with aliveness and I felt simultaneously deeply relaxed and keenly observant of my surroundings.

It was in the ancient city of Bagan, with over 2,000 temples and stupas, that I had the first in a series of what were unusually vivid dreams. On November 20th, I had the following dream:

I am in the house of a wealthy and beautiful witch. There are other women there, and she is giving things away—I can't tell if it is because she is about to die or she is already dead. She ushers me into her closet and gives me a pair of her shoes. Then she takes me into the living room, where a big picture of the tree of life is hanging over the couch. She shows it to me and then gives me a necklace that is fashioned into the shape of a pentagram. The necklace also worked like a homing device, and I am told my task is to tune into it and find the place that resonates the most by the tree of life. I find the place and it is revealed to me that I am a psychopomp and a seer into the otherworld.

When I woke up from this dream my entire body was pulsating with kundalini energy. I thought the specificity of the witch and pentagram and tree of life symbols to be very archetypal in nature, but also strange to me personally because I'd never had such images arise in my dreams before, let alone with such clarity.

In Jungian psychology, witches are an aspect of the archetype of the Mother. Traditionally, witches have a negative connotation, as in myriads of folk and fairytales in which an evil and dangerous witch attempts to victimize the young and vulnerable. Historically, women who were healers, mid-wives, or who were knowledgeable beyond culturally accepted levels, could be persecuted as witches. Yet, women have been taking back the power of the dark feminine. In a presentation at Pacifica Graduate Institute in June of 2017, depth psychologist Oksana Yakushko spoke of the power inherent in the image of the witch. She said, "The witch deals with mysterious and powers unknown . . . could it be the spirits or ancestors or maybe a meaningful calling to something we cannot yet see or know but have to face?" In the above dream, and others that I will detail soon, the witch seems to be leading me into a different dimension, a spiritual realm, and also suggesting that I acknowledge and use my own power. The witch leads me with a spiritual symbol of the pentagram, often associated with witches, to a symbol of the tree of life, another powerful archetypal symbol. I interpret this at least in part to connecting to a divine feminine source, and that the source is as ancient as the tree of life, is universal in nature, and is the divine Mother archetype.

The next day we traveled to Inle Lake. There people live in houses on stilts above the lake where they both fish and farm vegetables on gardens floating on the water, with the foothills of the Himalayas on the horizon. It was a beautiful, serene place, and we lodged that night on the edge of the lake. The night of November 21st I dreamed:

> I am in an insane asylum, though I know I'm not insane. I've been put here because I see things. I draw a picture that looks like scribbles to everyone else but I see it clearly. It is a picture of me. I am wearing a parka hood with fur around it. On top of the parka hood and on my head an eagle is perched, like a totem. Its wings hang on to either side of my head and it is looking into the distance. I have two sets of eyes. One pair is my regular eyes. One pair is in my forehead and when they open they are only dark pupils, no white or iris. These are my eyes that see into the otherworld. I see this in my drawing, but other people who don't have two sets of eyes just see a simple childish sketch of a girl. I look up from my drawing and I am suddenly looking into the otherworld and see a girl on a desolate path. She is alone and frightened. No one will go near her because she only has the second pair of seeing eyes, not regular eyes, and so she is shunned. I know I have to rescue her and so I have to break out of the asylum. There is also a young man in the asylum like me and the medical staff keeps medicating him to keep him quiet. I know I'm going to break out with him and we'll save the girl and then escape to Rasa House.

When I woke up from this dream, I was again suffused with shakti-kundalini energy. I related this dream to my husband, James, over breakfast, the shakti-kundalini still humming through my system. The sense of being able to see into another world was similar to the previous night's dream. Again, I felt surprised at the specificity of the images. The eagle, the two sets of eyes, one set that sees into the otherworld, and the girl on the path in the otherworld seemed very shamanic in their imagery.

This dream seemed to point to the unconscious attitude that if I claimed a feminine way of knowing, I would be considered crazy. This attitude (which has certainly been an attitude of Western culture for hundreds of years), was detrimental not only to the feminine self, but also to the male character in the dream, also imprisoned in the asylum. There was a need to break out of this attitude and rescue the more innocent aspect of the psyche represented by the girl, who was wholly visionary, and for that reason, cast out of culture and alone. I suspect this dream was not only personal in nature, but reflected the need for feminine, Eros ways of knowing to be rescued and reinstated as relevant to our culture.

On November 23rd, two nights later and still in Myanmar, I had the following dream:

> I am in Turkey with James and others whom I don't recognize. I am transported alone to the Hippodrome in Istanbul. I am on the far end of the track and a beautiful white stallion is thundering towards me from the opposite end. He reaches me and head-butts me and I fly through the air and land further from him, unharmed. As I get up from the ground the white horse is backing up, getting ready to head-butt me again. From out of the sky a witch dressed in all black flies down and grabs me. She scolds me and calls me an idiot because I did not realize the horse was going to kill me. The horse turns into a black demon horse with fangs and claws and wild eyes. The witch tells me to put my hands on the horse with her and together we chant an incantation. I assume we're doing it to calm the demon horse back into the white horse, but at the last moment the demon horse, with its claws and fangs, becomes stone, though we know it is still alive. Its hide has the same pattern that is on the soles of the Buddha's feet we see on the statues all over Myanmar—astrological symbols in a grid. The witch tells me to get on the horse and she gets on behind me, with her arms wrapped protectively around me, as if we're going to take off. Instead, the back of the horse opens like a portal, and we fall into and through the horse. I land by myself into a foggy, different world. It's dark and there is an old, dilapidated Victorian house in front of me, with graves in the front yard. It is almost a caricature of a haunted house scene from a movie. I think I should feel scared but I don't. I am walking towards the house when I wake up.

This was the third and last of the vivid dreams I had while I was in Myanmar. I didn't know what to make of them. The white horse, however, reminded me of Jung's dream of the hero Siegfried that he had to kill, as he realized that Siegfried represented his own personal will and heroic idealism and desire to have things his own way. Jung understood that there were higher states of consciousness than that of the ego, and it was necessary to respect these states, with the ego in service to them rather than trying to get its own way. Perhaps the white stallion represented something of my own ego that wanted to be pure, to charge ahead—but it also wanted to kill me, and it was a witch, all black in opposition to the white stallion, who saved me. It may also represent the conscious, intellectual, male-dominated attitude of the culture that would seem to be strong and beautiful, but in reality was murderous and even demonic. There seemed an oppositional dynamic of white and black, male and female. Even the location of Istanbul, on the borders of the Eastern and Western worlds, seemed to imply a bifurcation of energy. But it was the witch and an incantation that saved me from the demon horse, and the place I went was the otherworld, with a European Victorian home in the distance.

I want to pause here for a moment and look at the series of these images. Often in dreams there is a story-like trajectory over a period of time, as if the contents of the unconscious in unfolding like a mystery novel. As well, when images are repeated it often is like the unconscious is underlining a paragraph in a book, saying, "Hey! This is important, pay attention to this!" And lastly there is the numinous quality of the images from an embodied perspective since when I awoke I experienced realized the kundalini had been in the dream and continued to move through me even after the dream ended. The images were also what we would call archetypal is the classical sense: witches, the tree of life, pentagrams, even eagles and horses might be considered archetypal images in the collective unconscious. While the series of dreams were very curious to me in and of themselves, they would herald the beginnings of a further unfolding of the divine feminine that was yet to come.

The Goddess Comes Calling

When we returned to Jakarta and I continued working on my dissertation, I had the following dream:

I am talking to a scholarly woman friend of mine, and I'm telling her I want to go to the otherworld and bring back what I learned there in the form of stories. She tells me I should research Robert Graves.

Robert Graves was a vaguely familiar name but I didn't know who he was, so I looked him up and discovered he was a 19th century scholar, poet, and novelist. One of his most popular works was *The White Goddess*, which traces the history of the divine feminine back to goddess worship. In European culture, the divine feminine was recognized in her most archaic version as the triple goddess: maiden, mother, and crone. Synchronistically, several weeks later a friend spontaneously gifted me with a book, a compilation of feminist writers titled *Foremothers of the Women's Spirituality Movement: Elders and Visionaries*. My friend told me he felt intuitively it was something I should have. When I opened the book at random for a quick perusal, the first passage I read was by a woman whose first introduction to the divine feminine and goddess worship was by reading Robert Graves' book *The White Goddess*.

This was a very strong synchronicity. It was becoming clear that my research focusing on kundalini energy and personal transformation was missing something crucial—kundalini as a goddess or as an aspect of the divine feminine. Prior to this, I felt there was so much academic work on the divine feminine that I couldn't focus on that and kundalini in the same dissertation. Yet it was beginning to feel like the divine feminine was knocking on the door of my own psyche in dreams, demanding inclusion. What had been relegated to the otherworld, or the shadows of my own personal and perhaps cultural unconscious, was beginning to emerge.

In the beginning of 2016 I was on an annual month-long retreat with my spiritual group and teacher in Hawaii. During these retreats I would bring all my dissertation material to work on during afternoon breaks. In the last week of the retreat I had the following dream:

I am in a bedroom. My husband James is on a square bed in the center of the room. Something is alive and inside of him knocking around from the inside. I can see big lumps protruding from him as the being is trying to push out. James is scared but I keep saying "It's okay, it's Bhairava, it's Bhairava." I throw my arms around him to keep him calm and to transmit shakti energy to him. He suddenly turns to ashes in my arms, yet he still has form, but he looks like a burnt paper replica of himself. I tell people in the room to quickly place their hands on my husband as I breathe into his mouth. His ashen figure blows away as I blow into his mouth and what is revealed is a beautiful, exquisitely rendered statue of a goddess. She is in a golden Indian dress. Her skirt, top, and crown or headdress is fashioned out of gold, her skin is porcelain white, and her hair is blond. She has a serene, beatific expression on her face. I say, "Ah, this is the female Bhairava."

The name "Bhairava" refers to an earlier, more ancient name of Shiva. He is a fierce god, associated with annihilation. In my dream, my husband, and also Bhairava inside of him, is burnt to ashes and what remains is a female version of the god. Her demeanor is serene. She is made of alabaster and gold. The square bed in the center of the bedroom may indicate an unconscious urge towards wholeness through the transformation of energy from masculine to feminine, or a burning away of some thought structures around the masculine, revealing the feminine. The fact that it was also in classic Indian and Tantric imagery spoke to me of the divine feminine belonging to all realms, all religious and spiritual practices. I felt now it was crucial to include this aspect of the divine, with kundalini as the goddess representing the divine feminine.

The rest of 2016 was a period of deep transformation. Working on my dissertation while also participating in the teacher training was challenging. I felt I needed to be in California to practice the techniques given to me by my teacher and to work with the other teachers in the training program. In addition, we had a major renovation project on our home in California that I needed to oversee and I was beginning to organize participants for my dissertation research. I made the decision in May of 2016 to return to California while my husband remained in Jakarta completing the last year of his work before he could retire.

I moved into our home, empty of everything but a bed. I worked on getting settled, while also overseeing the outdoor renovation project, starting a part-time job, finishing my dissertation proposal, and even renovating an office space for myself for future work. It felt like my entire external life was mimicking some kind of internal renovation that was happening at a deep spiritual and psychological level. It was an exhausting, unsettled time, and I also missed my husband. With all the projects and changes, I felt I had bitten off more than I could chew, but at the same time I recognized that a new life was taking shape.

At the beginning of 2017, my dissertation proposal was approved and I also became initiated as a teacher in our spiritual practice in Ganeshpuri, India, by Swami Khecaranatha. Becoming a teacher meant that I would lead my own classes in the way that my teacher conducted them, by giving both open-eyed transmission of shakti as well as shakti by touch. When I came back to the United States in February, I set out quickly to find a place to teach and begin doing my participant interviews for my dissertation. However, it seemed that there was still more external transformation to come.

In the beginning of April, James called from Jakarta to tell me his retirement had been accelerated by six months. Since he had only one month to pack up and leave Jakarta, I flew back as soon as I could to help with the move, and I had to put my dissertation on hold. Just as I was launching into the second phase of my work it was postponed, and that felt meaningful in some way, but frustrating. The situation was out of my hands, and James and I had to manage the situation that was presented to us.

We returned to the States on May 15th, 2017. Settling in took time. All of our belongings from Jakarta arrived a month later. And then two weeks after that the contents of our storage unit from fourteen years prior when we left the United States arrived. Our house and garage were filled with boxes. Rummaging through the boxes of the past was a reflective process. James and I had been on a 14-year journey, living in Africa, Brazil, and Indonesia. James was beginning a new phase of his life in retirement; I was facing the first year of being a teacher and the first time I was to do my own independent research. A large chapter of our life had finished, and though there was so much to do to finally settle in, one could almost hear the door of the past gently click shut, and another creak open.

The Dead

During the second half of 2017 I conducted all my interviews. While I dreamed prolifically during this time, most of the dreams seemed unrelated to the interviews or the theme of the divine feminine, until September. On September 15th, I had two vivid dreams in one night. One dream was very clearly about the divine feminine, and one dream seemed to introduce a theme of the dead. It may be that the dreams of the dead, of speaking to the dead, were also related to the images and sense of the otherworld in my previous dreams. The dreams were as follows:

> I am with a small group from my spiritual practice and we were goofing around playing at a ritual of bringing in the dead. We were singing, walking, and dancing in a circle but people were not in rhythm or in tune, so I got more serious about leading the game and I instructed people to walk in rhythm and chant with purpose and focus. But one by one they seemed to fall down or get on the ground and curl up to go to sleep. This frustrated me, so I called out for the dead to not just appear to us but to rise within the bodies of the living. Several people in the circle stood up. They rose up but they were not wholly themselves. Their features and postures morphed, assuming the postures and features of the dead who had risen up inside them. I got very scared, thinking, "Uh oh! I can actually raise the dead!"

I woke up with a thundering heart. It was the middle of the night, and I was probably not fully awake, but it felt like I was very porous, as if the boundaries of my body were not solid, and that there were actually spirits entering and leaving my body, and I had no control over it. This frightened me even more and I prayed silently and intensely to Nityananda, the root lineage grandfather of our practice, for protection. As soon as I began my prayer my heart seemed to burst open with light and bliss. I felt surrounded and protected by a deep love, and I fell back to sleep. I slept for several hours more and then in the early dawn had the following dream:

> I am in my garden. There are plants growing that are strange and I don't know what they are. Areas of the garden seem to be yelling or scolding me because parts of it are dying and I have to find the cause. There is a big rose with deep roots that has been in the garden forever and she is like the mother plant; she is the primary entity telling me I need to save the garden. Then I see her main root is not

stable in the ground. I pull it towards me and the root completely comes out of the ground. The rose is in my hands and turns gray, shrivels, and becomes ash that blows away through my outstretched fingers. I am horrified and devastated because the mother rose was the heart of the garden, and if she dies things are very bad. If the garden dies, all will be lost.

This second dream had a profound impact on me. I felt deep grief that the mother rose had died in my dream for she felt like the Divine Mother herself dying. The dream haunted me, and in an attempt to go deeper in understanding of it, I meditated on the image, then I did a drawing of the rose, and finally I wrote a spontaneous poem with a journal entry after it, which gave me some sense of peace. This is the picture I drew and the poem and journal entry follow.

Divine Mother Rose

The Lineage

Something must die
for something else to be born.
Take up the mantle of voice.
Speak for the darkness,
for memory,
for the value of grief,
for the power inherent in silence,
in the cloak still unshed.
Speak to me of Me so that
I may be soothed in my long sleep.
Wake me so I can roar.

Journal Entry: "It is the Goddess who has sacrificed herself. It is the mother dying so her voice can be carried through to the next lineage holders. She is asking me to be a voice, to know my own garden and soul so that it thrives in feminine wisdom. To hold the darkness, the otherworld, the ancestors, to see in the dark and bring the darkness back, to soothe the light with soul, with the cooling hand of the mother."

The spontaneous drawing and writing had a calming effect on me. I was a bit surprised by what I wrote, particularly about the ancestors. Were the dead of the previous dream the ancestors? Jung said of the image of the rose that it was often a metaphor for Mary, or like the lotus in Indian culture, both of which represent the divine feminine. In my unconscious, there seemed an urgent push towards understanding what was in my own garden, my own soul, and that to fail to do so would be the death of the feminine.

Not long after that, while meditating with my spiritual community, I had a very strong sense of hearing a voice, not an audible voice but rather as if someone was typing out a clear, matter-of-fact message in my mind, and it said, "You ARE the dead." This was disconcerting to say the least. I had a sudden desire to go see my doctor. I could not discern with any certainty what that might mean, but my sense was that my consciousness in meditation as well as in my dreams was beginning to tune in to a more collective level rather than personal level of experience.

According to Jung, the level of the collective unconscious is where all of humanity's memories reside, from the beginning of time. A few weeks later, on November 15th, I had the following dream:

> A handsome older man, perhaps in his late 60s, is sleeping in a single bed. A beautiful, fierce, otherworldly-looking Goddess is behind him, and his head is actually lying in her lap. She is brown-skinned with a high pile of black hair, like the ancient Egyptian queen Nefertiti. She is very thin and she has beautiful bracelets and jewelry adorning her arms. She has incredibly long fingers and she is touching his head and temples, sending energy into his brain. Then she flies into the air and her body changes. She is less human now, and she has magnificent, curling horns that are striped black and white coming out of her temples. She makes a fierce kind of screeching and takes a sword and decapitates the man. I'm shocked, and she tells me it must be done. I know then that it is not a bad thing because all this energy can now be released out of his head.

When I woke up from this dream I sensed the lingering presence of this goddess right behind me, as if I were the old man with my head in her lap. I had the impression of her fingers still pressing on my temples and there was a great deal of shakti-kundalini running through my body. From an alchemical perspective, this might be considered an initiation dream, the slaying of the old king, like the Fisher King, so that a new energy can emerge. Jung wrote of the alchemical significance of decapitation as a sacrificial act in service to alchemical transformation.

Two weeks later, on November 29th, a dream seemed to indicate an alchemical process was working:

> I am in Bali with the actor Matthias Schoenaerts. We are in an apartment with a TV, but when the TV is on it leaks water outside. I go outside to check the leak and the ground is saturated and caving in. The caving-in revealed a small tunnel of earth and leaves, and through the tunnel I can see the sea. Matthias is shoveling off the fallen earth. He has revealed a set of steps going down to the ocean. These steps take me down to an open, grassy area.

143

Beautiful flowers are planted all the way down the stairs and I know there will be a wedding. Everything is exquisite. I go inside a building that somehow feels like the room in which Nityananda died in Ganeshpuri, India. There is a woman on a throne with people around her. She is me, but I also watch her. Then someone goes to a back room and gets animal blood and dumps it over the woman's head. I am furious. Then the dream scene changes and the two dream women, who I realize in the dream were also me, are outside looking at the sea. I am enraged at her for dumping blood all over me and I'm going to kill her. I leapt on her and began to strangle her but she didn't care, she didn't fight. She just kept saying over and over again that she was going to get married. I knew she would marry Matthias Schoenarerts. I wanted to stay angry but she was so happy that the anger and the fight drained out of me instantly.

The feeling in the dream was one of deep beauty and grace that felt very sacred. It seemed to suggest that an alchemical marriage, or *coniunctio*, was to happen soon. The actor Matthias Schoenarerts often plays strongly masculine roles, perhaps indicating and animus figure in my psyche. The dousing in blood might indicate the integration of the in-stinctive element with the spiritual element, and it appeared that initially I misunderstood this act. But as the dream ended, my ego dream self was won over by the sheer joy of the impending marriage. I was interested to see where my dreams would go next, and if a marriage, an alchemical wedding, would take place soon. I was also curious that these dreams were progressing without anything in my external, conscious life seeming to be a causal factor impacting the dreams. I was continuing to teach meditation classes and work on my dissertation. Teaching meditation weekly revved up the kundalini energy running through my system. Some nights after teaching I had a hard time sleeping because of so much energy. Some mornings when I woke up it felt like a fire hydrant of water had blown through my heart, leaving it purified and wide open. It is possible that this additional energy was impacting my deeper psyche and revealed itself and its progression through my dream life.

In January of 2018, I was in Hawaii at our annual meditation retreat for three weeks. During this time I meditated four times a day and also worked on the participant interviews for this dissertation. In the last week of my retreat, January 23rd, I had the following dream:

> I am at Rasa House with James and some friends. It's 4:30 in the morning and James is in the living room. I come out to greet him, and I look out the window, surprised it is light enough to see outside. Two beautiful stags are grazing in the partial snow as the snow is melting and revealing green patches of grass. They have magnificent, full antlers. I point them out to James, and as I do, two more stags appear. One seems to be wearing a little Santa hat with bells on it and a silver garland in its antlers. I was baffled at how a wild deer had gotten decorations in his antlers, but he seemed unperturbed. My friends go out of the house. One of them goes to a wedding happening next door. James and I go out to look for them and notice many people hiking on our property. The friends return and we are all standing on the front deck. We see that a Gingko tree has grown through the slats of the deck. It is young and had pushed the deck slats aside. It has beautiful golden leaves, and small white flowers. I was surprised it was blooming in winter. Someone tells me it will bloom much more in the warmer seasons. I see a wall with colorful flowers draped over it. Nathaji has put them there. I know that there will be more flowers coming in the summer.

What struck me most about the dream were the four stags and the Gingko tree. Stags have many mythological and archetypally symbolic meanings. In *The Grail Legend*, by Emma Jung and Marie-Louise von Franz, the stag is a symbol of God, of the Self of Jung's individuation process. Because there are four stags in this dream, and one has celebratory decorations of Christmas, or the birth of Christ, one might view the stags as relating more closely with a sense of impending wholeness of the Self.

The Gingko tree is the most ancient of all trees. Scientists estimate that the Gingko tree has survived with relatively little change to its DNA structure for over two hundred million years. In the East, it is a symbol of longevity, hope, and peace. I remembered back to the tree of life in the dream I had of the beautiful witch who gave me a pentagram necklace. The tree is also a sacred symbol in the Celtic tradition.

A week later, when we had returned home from retreat to California, I had the following dream:

> I'm in India, which is somehow also Hawaii, in a huge castle that is built like a fortress. Nathaji is also there and he is meditating. As he meditates he channels Nityananda. When Nathaji opens his eyes they are completely black, without the whites, and I know that means Nityananda is present. Nityananda wants to give me a gift, which manifests in Nathaji's hand. It's a large oak tree. It is full grown with large branches above and roots below connected to a thick trunk, but it is in its dormant winter phase. The scene changes and I am telling a friend who often works with dreams about a dream I had in which the Goddess merged with me and told me I WAS the goddess. My friend rolls her eyes in a humorous way, like she is saying, "Duh!" Simultaneously as I am telling her about the dream of merging with the Goddess, I see the goddess behind me walk into and merge with me. The telling of the dream to my friend and the experience of the Goddess merging with me happen concurrently. I feel this incredible bliss and I turn into a butterfly, but I'm so enormous my wings undulate like a manta ray's. I fly around in euphoria in an orange, pink, and golden sunrise, like I'm having a joy ride of bliss in the merging of myself with the Goddess, and then I come back down and transform back into a human body.

This dream again seemed to suggest a merging, or *coniunctio,* between the divine feminine and my own human state. Once again there was a symbol of the tree, this time offered as a gift from the grandfather of my spiritual lineage. Since the tree symbol and the goddess appear in the same dream, I understood that both the Tantric lineage and the divine feminine could be equally integrated in my experience. Both were part of a larger whole of my psyche. With the goddess merging with my own body, it seemed that psyche, as symbolized by the butterfly, was liberated and joyous. Butterflies are also archetypal symbols of transformation, as they change from worm, to chrysalis, to butterfly. In this dream it was my body, merged with the divine feminine, that transformed into a butterfly, into an ecstatic psyche, and then transformed back again into my human body.

Dream Reflections

In my story thus far, I provided many potential connections with symbolic imagery and their associations. I suggested possible archetypal associations with the images themselves and also to psychological alchemical processes. The Jungian analyst Thom Cavalli in his book *Alchemical Psychology: Old Recipes for Living in a New World*, wrote, "The imaginal world remains rooted in our neural makeup, representing a different time and place, connecting us to our origins and perhaps even our collective soul."[38] Perhaps being told in a dream that I followed the old ways was indicative of a larger psychic process to integrate the collective soul into my individual sense of soul and self, and to mediate my own unconscious material in relationship with my conscious self. I believe the energy of kundalini was facilitating the movement of unconscious psychic material across the boundaries of the imaginal world and the conscious world. I'm not implying that one must experience kundalini as such to have experiences of diving into the unconscious and imaginal dimensions, but rather it is an additional fuel and tool that augments and enriches the process.

One may also notice in my dreams the continued evolution of the feminine energy evolving from witch images to Goddess images as a progression in psyche. Though I never experienced the witches as evil as they have often been denoted culturally throughout the centuries, they were in the shadow—dark, mysterious, unknown, and unconscious. Over time the images progressed to a female Bhairava, who was serene and beautiful, yet passive, but ultimately much lighter and more clearly of a divine origin. Then the image progressed to a rose, albeit with a warning that I must do the work of tending to my own garden, my own psyche and soul, if the connection was not to be lost.

Lastly there were three dreams and one synchronicity I had in this dream series that I'll describe here because they seem to illustrate this sense of internalizing and integrating a previously projected energy. In the first dream:

> I am walking down a plain, unadorned hallway. At the end of the hall is a door. I come to it and I already know that when I open it the Goddess will be there. I open the door and I see her, but her back is to me. She has long, dark, very curly hair. She turns around to smile at me and at first she just looks like a regular person, but as her smile deepens her eyes flash a brilliant, peridot green. The power coming out of her is love, but it is so strong and fierce that my knees are buckling under me and I can barely look at her. I begin to wake up, and as I do I feel the shakti-kundalini rising in me from my feet upwards, like water filling a vessel. As it reaches the level of my heart, it turns the same brilliant green as her eyes and I fully wake into bliss.

I realized later that the green of her eyes and the green of the shakti at the level of my heart is identical to the color green traditionally shown as the heart chakra.

The next two dreams happened within a week of each other and are related to the synchronicity I'll describe after the dreams. On May 16th I dreamed:

> I'm on a field trip or vacation somewhere that feels like Europe. We end up in an open field, but it's craggy as well, like being in the Scottish Highlands. We are going to set up a picnic or a camp on the flat plain we are on, but looking up at the towering mountains behind us, I can see an old fortress built into the mountains and it looks much more interesting so we decide to set ourselves up there.

On May 25th I dreamed:

> I'm at a retreat with my spiritual group and Nathaji. A friend in the group shows me his house, which is palatial and dug right into the mountain. I am stunned by how big it is and he invites me to check it out. We find ourselves in the open, tiled courtyard of the palace. The floor is beautifully tiled. Then we go back to the retreat.

Five days later, on May 30th I was reading news online. There was a travel article on places to go in Eastern Europe. The article mentioned Montenegro as a destination, and suggested visiting the Ostrog Monastery. The photos of the monastery caused the hairs on my arms to rise. It looked exactly like the place in my dreams. It was built into a cliff face, had a large open courtyard, and below was a craggy but flat plain. The monastery was founded by and dedicated to St. Basil, and one of the major pilgrimage festivals each year is dedicated to the presentation of the Virgin Mary. The Virgin Mary is yet another archetypal image of the divine feminine.

This last synchronicity with dream images continues to reinforce the importance of the divine feminine in my life, and it is through my work over the years with kundalini that such a connection has evolved. It is through Jungian and archetypal work that I am able to engage the images with open curiosity and respect.

I am grateful for the direction of my dreams at the time of my doctoral research, and I am deeply grateful for the direct and continuous experience of shakti-kundalini that guides me always deeper into my psyche and Self. The dream images that were often culturally Western in orientation co-exist with my Eastern practice. For me, the divine feminine is present as part of the cosmic, sacred whole, regardless of one's spiritual tradition.

CONCLUSION

Striking the Match

I hope that the stories I've shared in the previous chapters have been thought-provoking and have given you an opportunity to contemplate the spiritual experiences of kundalini in others while also encouraging your own personal reflections. Truthfully, I wish I were sitting next to you, listening and witnessing your reactions. Did you find yourself nodding in recognition in parts? Did you see your own kundalini experiences and/or those of others you know reflected in these stories? Did you dream more as you read more? Did you notice synchronicities occurring? And what happened in your body as you read?

I ask about the sensations in your body because one of the unique qualities of a numinous kundalini experience is its physical, palpable presence in and on the body. We know we're having a kundalini experience first and foremost because our body knows it. Each body experiences kundalini uniquely, and yet there is also an archetypal felt experience in the body that identifies what's happening as kundalini. I invite you to sense into some of the embodied descriptors used by the participants in this book: *weighty, subtle, dense, pulsating, moving, jolting, upward, downward, spinning, surging, energized, bursting, light, popping, ringing, flowing, tingling, speedy, rushes, orgasmic, delicious, melting, blissful, heat.*

In these descriptions we sense the dynamism and aliveness of the kundalini experience. To the sensing body, kundalini has mass, weight, directionality, movement, and even temperature. It's as if the body is the encasement for a living, electrical force, and yet the body is not just an inert receptacle for the energy—rather it engages and responds to the kundalini energy.

In my experience working with kundalini for almost 30 years, I have come to recognize that how kundalini is experienced in the body can change over time. It may be experienced in different parts of the body, with varying degrees of intensity and sensations. What makes it discernable as kundalini and not another kind of physical sensation or set of symptoms is a sense of intelligent presence. It can be felt throughout the body, not just within the chakra system. It is often accompanied by a profound sense of love and ecstasy—a breathtaking Eros—and it opens the psyche to a larger and deeper sense of connection to the cosmos. It is an energy that can be cultivated through practice, but it also has its own directional radar of which the ego has no control. The practice of opening to the energy, not attempting to control it, allows the energy to flow with more ease and intensity, and this intensity, in turn, may gradually bring about the flowering of psyche into its own full wholeness.

Igniting the Flame

I want to tell you a little secret about kundalini. Kundalini is catching! This doesn't mean you'll catch it unknowingly like a cold, but rather kundalini is a flame that can ignite other flames. Like a candle tipped from one wick to another, the energy enlivened in one person may in turn enliven another. In his book *The Secret Teaching of Plants*, plant researcher and poet Stephen Harrod Buhner wrote about the electromagnetic field of the human heart, and specifically pointed to certain organic cells called "pacemaker cells" (not to be confused with the mechanical device inserted into the heart, the pacemaker, named after these cells). Alone, one pacemaker cell will lose its pattern, but if two pacemaker cells are next to each other, their rhythmic patterns of pulsation will synchronize and then begin to beat in unison, even if they're not touching. Essentially, a healthy cell will entrain a non-healthy cell to its own pattern.

In Tantric practices, the transfer of shakti energy to a person is called *shaktipat* or *diksa*. The transmission of energy enlivens the energy of kundalini from someone who is an adept to someone whose kundalini can be further encouraged. Traditionally this happens in four ways: through look, touch, word, and thought. On one level, I believe this process is a kind of entrainment, a coming into rhythm between two energy systems. We might say it is the electromagnetic field of the heart of the subtle body that begins to synchronize and fall into a similar rhythm. Buhner noted that the heart "produces a tremendously powerful, broadband electromagnetic field as it beats,"[39] and this electromagnetic field of the entire human body "aligns roughly along a person's spine, from the pelvic floor to the top of the skull. This field permeates every cell in the body."[40] This description seems remarkably similar to the description in Tantra of the sushumna channel, which corresponds to the spinal column, and the structure of the chakra system that begins at the base of the spine and terminates at the crown of the head.

In reading these stories, perhaps you began to feel a sense of falling into rhythm with them, feeling your body or your heart respond in kind, relaxing in, and simultaneously being curious about, that sense of flow. And perhaps not—either experience is perfectly fine. But maybe you're wondering after reading this book, "What next?"

Creating the Fire

The answer to that question depends on what you're interested in. In the pages that follow, I'll provide you with some additional books to read on Tantra, kundalini, Jung, and the Divine Feminine. If you want to do further research, you may choose to track down some of the references in this book, or if you want a really deep dive, you could download my dissertation from the database Proquest (a local librarian should be able to help with that). If you're looking for more practical, "hands-on" engagement, I'll list a few resources you might check out for classes or more immersive study. If you feel like you're having your own kundalini awakening and need some guidance, there are resources for that too.

This is as far as we can travel together in this book you hold in your hands or engage with on the screen. But before we go, I want to leave you with one last image that came to mind as I worked with the stories of Ryan, Colleen, Jeremy, and Maria, as well as my own. I thought of our stories as the stories of contemporary everyday mystics, each with our unique archetypal resonances. I kept thinking of the final scene of the movie *The Breakfast Club*, when the five main characters come out of the high school building after their day of detention. We hear the voice of nerdy Brian Johnson reading from the essay he wrote, in which he says they, the detained students, are seen in the simplest of terms as the brain, the athlete, the basket case, the criminal, and the princess. He's speaking of stereotypes of course, but there is also archetypal resonance to each of those roles. If you would for me, queue up in your mind the Simple Minds' theme song of the movie, "Don't You Forget about Me." In your imaginal psyche picture us, the five storytellers in this book: a rebel, a warrior, a lover, an artist, and a scholar. We are these things, and yet each of us embodies a bit of each other's archetypal energy as well, brought together through our shared mystical experience of kundalini. Perhaps you are realizing or beginning to accept and own that mystical part of yourself, the very home of your being, with its own unique archetypal quality, or perhaps you are already quite at home there, and have had your own unforgettable experiences of kundalini. Regardless of your experience level, you are one of us now, by virtue of engaging with our stories, and if you were sitting next to me here at the conclusion of this book, I would want to hear your story as well. And then I would assure you: we are not simple minds, nor are we singular. We're all part of the tree of life, and when the light breaks through, we are all held in the vital and loving field of Shakti-Kundalini.

RESOURCES

Books

C. G. Jung and Depth Psychology

There are hundreds of books by Jung and about Jung and Jungian psychology. You can check the endnotes section of this book to see some of the titles I used for research, but I'll list a few more here that are especially relevant to kundalini.

Jung, C. G. (1963). *Memories, dreams, reflections.* A. Jaffé (Ed.). New York, NY: Random House.

> This is Jung's memoir, and it's a way to peek into his mind and times and see how he formulated his psychology. He also chronicled some of his own trials and tribulations with spiritual experiences.

Clarke, J. J. (1994). *Jung and Eastern thought: A dialogue with the Orient.* London: Routledge.

> Clarke offered a nice comparison of Indian philosophy and Jungian thought.

Edinger, E. F. (1985). *Anatomy of the psyche: Alchemical symbolism in psychotherapy.* La Salle, IL: Open Court.

> Edinger broke down the alchemical stages from the original writings to the modern day experience in dreams and psychotherapy.

Jung, C. G. (1996). *The psychology of kundalini yoga: Notes of the seminar given in 1932 by C. G. Jung.* S. Shamdasani (Ed.). Princeton, NJ: Princeton University Press.

> While many of Jung's notions in this transcription of his seminar lectures is quite dated, and comes from an intellectual, analytical perspective rather than from direct experience, it provides a sense of Jung's interest and thoughts on the kundalini.

Tantric Philosophy and Practice

More books continue to become available on Tantra, particularly as many of the original works are found and translated. I'll list just a few here, as the authors were also noted in the text of this book.

Wallis, C. D. (2012). *Tantra illuminated: The philosophy, history, and practice of timeless tradition.* Petaluma, CA: Mattamayura Press.

> This is a comprehensive and accessible book on the history and practice of Tantra from its inception to contemporary practices.

Khecaranatha, S. (2013). *Shiva's trident: The consciousness of freedom and the means to liberation.* Berkeley, CA: Prasad Press.

> Swami Khecaranatha wrote about integrating kundalini into everyday life in a very down-to-earth voice. He has many books available through Amazon.

Kundalini rising: Exploring the energy of awakening. (2009). Boulder, CO: Sounds True.

> This is a compilation of scholars and scientists who look at kundalini from various perspectives.

Greenwell, B. (1995). *Energies of transformation: A guide to the kundalini process.* Saratoga, CA: Shakti River Press.

> While this is a slightly older book, it has great information on

kundalini, from its collective cultural roots, to the experiences them-selves. This book developed out of Greenwell's own dissertation research on the subject.

The Divine Feminine

The subject of the divine feminine has a rich variety of authors and perspectives, too many for me to do the subject any justice. Below is a short list of some of my favorites, and ones that have a depth psychological or mythological perspective.

Austen, H. I. (1990). *The heart of the goddess: Art, myth and meditations of the world's Sacred Feminine.* Berkeley, CA: Wingbow Press.

> This is a beautiful book of images of the goddess from various cultures and epochs. Each image comes with a description of the goddess with a poem or meditation that can be used for your own contemplations.

Bolen, J. S. (1994). *Crossing to Avalon: A woman's midlife quest for the sacred feminine.* New York, NY: Harper One.

> This is a memoir by the psychiatrist and Jungian analyst Jean Shinoda Bolen, chronicling her personal quest to find the sacred feminine. It's an engaging and archetypal journey, and readers may both enjoy Bolen's quest and find personal resonance with their own journeys.

Gimbutas, M. (1999). *The living goddesses.* Berkeley, CA: University of California Press.

> Gimbutas shocked the male-dominated field of archeology with her own well-researched work on the goddess throughout cultures and history. This book is a compilation of her many years of research on the subject and spans a rich diversity of regions and images.

Perera, S. B. (1981). *Descent to the goddess: A way of initiation for women.* Toronto, Canada: Inner City Books.

This slim little book packs a punch. Perara used the ancient Sumerian myth of the Goddess Inanna-Ishtar to illustrate an archetypal process of descent and initiation for women that speaks to our modern times.

Resources for Practice and Support

It's always crucial to check out a teacher or a practice thoroughly before committing to engagement. Make sure the teacher is vetted by someone you respect and be certain that his or her teaching resonates with your heart. This is a short list of teachers that I have worked with either personally or with their online material, and I feel that they have great integrity, knowledge, and personal, direct experience.

Swami Khecaranatha and Heart of Consciousness:
https://heartofc.org

Lawrence Edwards:
http://anamcara-ny.org

Christopher Wallis and the Tantrika Institute:
https://tantrikainstitute.org

If you are needing additional support or feel that you are going through a spiritual crisis, you may find assistance through these websites:

Spiritual Emergence Network:
http://www.spiritualemergence.org

The International Spiritual Emergence Network:
https://www.spiritualemergencenetwork.org

And you can always reach me at www.danaswainphd.com.

ACKNOWLEDGMENTS

After writing a dissertation, the thought of taking the same material that I had researched, organized, and sweated over for several years and turning it into a book didn't initially appeal to me. Two things changed my mind: the number of people who found my dissertation online and wrote to me telling me that it helped them, and my publisher, Dr. Jennifer Leigh Selig. Jennifer was also the head of my dissertation committee, and she treated this book project and me with the same steady patience, encouragement, and keen editing eye as she did with my dissertation. Without her, this book would never have been birthed.

A heart-felt thank you to the participants who allowed me to include their stories in this book. Their courage and openness in sharing their experiences with me not only made the work possible but also illustrated the depth and breadth of opportunities for growth offered through kundalini. Each story was as unique as the individuals themselves.

To my friends and family who relentlessly asked and gently prodded me with the casual (and not so casual) question: "How's the book going?" I thank you for never letting me off the hook or wander too far from my path and goal.

My profound gratitude goes to Swami Khecaranatha (Nathaji), who is interwoven into the heart and spirit and lives of many of these stories, including my own. As a true teacher you show me every day how to walk with integrity and dedication in service to my deepest self. It is an honor and a profound grace to have walked the spiritual path with you as my guide.

My deepest gratitude and love to my husband James for always making space for my dreams in our life together. Your generosity of spirit as I followed my own call was, and is, remarkable. I could not imagine a better partner to share my thoughts, dreams, visions, and life with. Thank you.

ENDNOTES

[1] Merton, T. (1960). *The wisdom of the desert: Sayings from the desert fathers of the fourth century.* New York, NY: New Directions Publishing Corporation, p. 11.

[2] Jung, C. G. (1969b). *Aion: Researches into the phenomenology of the self.* Princeton. N.J.: Princeton University Press. (Original work published in 1959), p. 40.

[3] White, D. G. (1996). *The alchemical body: Siddha traditions in medieval India.* Chicago, IL: University of Chicago Press, p. 208.

[4] Ray, R. A. (2008). *Touching enlightenment: Finding realization in the body.* Boulder, CO: Sounds True, p. 25.

[5] Ibid, p. 24.

[6] Sannella, L. (1987). *The kundalini experience: Psychosis or transcendence?* Lower Lake, CA: Integral Publishing, p. 23.

[7] Ibid, p. 104.

[8] Silburn, L. (1988). *Kundalini: The energy of the depths: A comparative study based on the scriptures of nondualistic Kasmir Saivism.* Albany, NY: State University of New York Press, p. 26.

[9] Louchakova, O. (2009). Kundalini and health: Living well with spiritual awakening. In *Kundalini rising: Exploring the energy of awakening* (pp. 97-115). Boulder, CO: Sounds True, p. 104.

[10] Goodchild, V. (2006). Psychoid, psychophysical, P-subtle! Alchemy and a new worldview. *Spring: A Journal of Archetype and Culture, 74,* 63-88, p. 67.

[11] Jung, as cited in Goodchild, V. (2006). Psychoid, psychophysical, P-subtle! Alchemy and a new worldview. *Spring: A Journal of Archetype and Culture, 74,* 63-88, p. 68.

[12] von Franz, M.-L. (1992). *Psyche and matter.* Boston, MA: Shambhala, p. 176.

[13] Jung, C. G. (1968). Psychology and alchemy. In H. Read, et al. (Eds.), *The collected works of C. G. Jung* (R. F. C. Hull, Trans.) (Vol. 12, 2nd

ed.) London: Routledge and Kegan Paul. (Original work published in 1953), p. 279.

[14] Jung, C. G. (1969). The structure and dynamics of the psyche. In H. Read, et al.(Eds). *The collected works of C. G. Jung* (R.F.C. Hull, Trans.) (Vol. 8). Princeton, NJ: Princeton University Press. (Original work published in 1960), p. 21.

[15] Goodchild, V. (2006). Psychoid, psychophysical, P-subtle! Alchemy and a new worldview. *Spring: A Journal of Archetype and Culture, 74*, 63-88, p. 82.

[16] Ibid.

[17] Bohm, D. (2003). *The essential David Bohm.* L. Nichol (Ed.). London: Routledge, p. 80.

[18] Ibid, p. 85.

[19] Ibid, p. 86.

[20] Newberg, A. (2009). The yogic brain. In *Kundalini rising: Exploring the energy of awakening* (pp. 117-125). Boulder, CO: Sounds True, p. 120.

[21] Harris Whitfield, B. (2009). Mental and emotional health in the kundalini process. In *Kundalini rising: Exploring the energy of awakening.* Boulder, CO: Sounds True, p. 150.

[22] Jung, C. G. (1966). Psychology and religion: West and east. In H. Read, M. Fordham, G. Adler, & W. McGuire (Eds.), *The collected works of C. G. Jung* (R. F. C. Hull, Trans.). (Vol. 11). Princeton, NJ: Princeton University Press. (Original work published in 1938), p. 492.

[23] Abhinavagupta. (2015). *Abhinavagupta's tantraloka and other works* (Vol. 2) (S. P. Singh & S. Maheshvarananda, Trans.). New Delhi: Standard, p. xxxii.

[24] Mahaffey, P. (2013). Self-inquiry in C. G. Jung's depth psychology and Hindu yoga traditions. *Spring: A Journal of Archetype and Culture,* (90), 125-151, p. 144.

[25] Clarke, J. J. (1994). *Jung and Eastern thought: A dialogue with the Orient.* London: Routledge, p. 112.

[26] Mahaffey, P. (2013). Self-inquiry in C. G. Jung's depth psychology and Hindu yoga traditions. *Spring: A Journal of Archetype and Culture,* (90), 125-151, p. 147.

[27] Hillman, J. (1985). *Anima: An anatomy of a personified notion.* Dallas, TX: Spring Publications, p. 53.

[28] Abhinavagupta. (2015). *Abhinavagupta's tantraloka and other works* (Vol. 2) (S. P. Singh & S. Maheshvarananda, Trans.). New Delhi: Standard, p. xxxi.

[29] Silburn, L. (1988). *Kundalini: The energy of the depths: A comparative study based on the scriptures of nondualistic Kasmir Saivism.* Albany, NY: State University of New York Press, p. 137.

[30] von Franz, M.-L. (1992). *Psyche and matter.* Boston, MA: Shambhala, p. 142.

[31] Perry, J. W. (1999). *Trials of the visionary mind: Spiritual emergency and the renewal process.* Albany, NY: State University of New York Press, p. 135.

[32] Shankarananda, S. (2003). *The yoga of Kashmir Shaivism: Consciousness is everything.* Delhi: Motilal Banarsidass, p. 42.

[33] Ibid, p. 42.

[34] Assagioli, R. (2007). *Transpersonal development: The dimension beyond psychosynthesis.* Findhorn: Inner Way Productions, pp. 121-122.

[35] Kalsched, D. (2013). *Trauma and the soul: A psycho-spiritual approach to human development and its interruption.* London: Routledge, p. 5.

[36] Jung, C. G. (1969). The archetypes and the collective unconscious. In H. Read et al. (Eds.) *The collected works of C. G. Jung* (R. F. C. Hull, Trans.) (Vol. 9, Part 1). Princeton, NJ: Princeton University Press. (Original work published in 1959), p. 18.

[37] Kalsched, D. (1996). *The inner world of trauma: Archetypal defenses of the personal spirit.* Hove: Routledge, p. 3.

[38] Cavalli, T. (2002). *Alchemical psychology: Old recipes for living in a new world.* New York, NY: Putnam, p. 106.

[39] Buhner, S. H. (2004). *The secret teachings of plants: The intelligence of the heart in the direct perception of nature.* Rochester, VT: Bear, p. 86.

[40] Ibid, p. 87.

Printed in Great Britain
by Amazon